Y0-BUK-822

Legal Almanac Series No. 77

HOW TO COPE WITH UNITED STATES CUSTOMS

by Arthur I. Demcy, L.L.B., L.L.M.
   Member of New York Bar
   Member of U.S. Customs Bar
   U.S. Customs Consultant
   Formerly U.S. Customs Examiner
      of Books and Printed Matter

1976 OCEANA PUBLICATIONS, INC.
Dobbs Ferry, New York

To My Wife Reggie

ACKNOWLEDGMENT

My grateful thanks are due to Bernard Klein, Deputy Assistant
Regional Commissioner of Customs; Seton E. Gilbert, Methods
and Standards Analyst, U.S. Postal Service; and Hy Cole,
formerly U.S. Customs Inspector, for their helpful cooperation.

This is the seventy-seventh in a series of LEGAL ALMANACS which bring you
the law on various subjects in nontechnical language. These books do not take
the place of your attorney's advice, but they can introduce you to your legal rights
and responsibilities.

Library of Congress Cataloging in Publication Data

Demcy, Arthur I   1904-
   How to cope with United States Customs.

   (Legal almanac series; no. 77)
   "Trade act of 1974": p.
   1. Customs administration—United States.
2. Customs administration and tourists—United States.
I. United States.   Laws, statutes, etc.   Trade act of 1974.
1976.   II. Title.
HJ6622.D45   352'.13   76-16154
ISBN 0-379-11103-9

TABLE OF CONTENTS

INTRODUCTION

How does one cope with United States Customs? By being realistic! The mental attitudes of both traveler or tourist and the customs inspector should be sound on judgment in that each should emphasize mutual agreement and minimize differences. We are emotional beings with passions and should resort to effective thinking to overcome any obstacle that may ensue.

The customs inspector has certain defined duties to perform; he is authorized to search and detain persons violating customs and other laws. He collects the revenue and penalties due on imported articles. He is our first line of defense against contraband smuggling and illegal entry of merchandise, and articles which are detrimental to our health. He renders many other functions for our government, cooperating with as many as forty various agencies as a law enforcement officer or assisting these agencies to fulfill their tasks.

Today we have both male and female inspectors. They go through special training whereby they obtain their knowledge of the rules, regulations, and procedures in compliance with the administrative provisions of the tariff. Applied psychology, a very important subject, is taken during the course and helps them to understand the actions and reactions of their supervisors, their coworkers and particularly the public.

As a rule, customs inspectors are polite, courteous, and devoted to their duties. It is common knowledge that most people who travel abroad or import merchandise are imbued with the customary distaste for paying duties. There are, of course, a few exceptions—those who try to deprive our government of its revenue. These are the people who brag about their accomplishments should they succeed in their fraudulent maneuvers. However, they soon learn the risk is not worthwhile, compared to the penalty if caught in the unlawful act. The trickery or device that is used by the exceptional tourist or traveler in the art of subterfuge is very easily detected by the customs inspector.

When the customs inspector wants to make a thorough search of your baggage, don't feel offended or angry with him. There is no need to be fearful or prejudiced either. All these prejudgments arise before you consider any evidence of his actions.

Every job has its trials and tribulations and so does the customs inspector's! So, try to cooperate. It is feasible to have a bill on hand for your purchases abroad. It is also expedient to collect your purchases and place them where they are easily available for examination. Here are some of the "don'ts."

1. Don't insist that the seller of the article place a lower price on the bill rather than the true amount you paid.
2. Don't claim that some of the articles were used whereas in reality they are new.
3. Don't have artists falsify documents that works of art are originals whereas they are reproductions in order to import them free of duty.
4. Don't have sellers of antiquities issue a false statement giving the date of manufacture within 100 years in order to avoid payment of duty.
5. Don't accept a package from a stranger to deliver to a friend in the states in consideration for a certain fee. Unknowingly, you might be a party to smuggling narcotics or other contraband.

If the customs inspector is not satisfied with your declaration or your invoice as to value, he is justified in applying Sec. 500 of the Tariff Act of 1930 as amended.

The appropriate customs officer will under rules and regulations prescribed by the secretary of the treasury:

1. appraise merchandise in the unit of quantity in which the merchandise is usually bought and sold by ascertaining or estimating the value thereof by all reasonable ways and means in his power, any statement of cost or costs of production in any invoice, affidavit, declaration, or other document to the contrary notwithstanding;
2. ascertain the classification and rate of duty applicable to such merchandise;
3. fix the amount of duty to be paid on such merchandise and determine any increased or additional duties due or any excess of duties deposited;
4. liquidate the entry of such merchandise; and
5. give notice of such liquidation to the importer, his

consignee, or agent in such form and manner as
the secretary shall prescribe in such regulations.

The purpose of this book is to provide guidance so that
travelers and tourists may take advantage of privileges of
which they may be unaware, also to guide potential importers,
including institutions, who lack experience in the activity of
importing merchandise.

Chapter 1

THE CREATION OF THE U.S. CUSTOMS SERVICE

The word "tariff" could easily be linked to the word "tribute," which reverts to ancient times. Reluctance to pay was quite prevalent and led to either duress or smuggling. During the Revolutionary Period, the colonists deemed it a grave hardship to cope with the British and the taxes the British inflicted on them. In order to overcome this barrier they finally resolved that they would resort to smuggling. The British, very much aware of this, resorted to severe punitive measures by introducing the Sugar Act, which insisted on the payment of duties on lumber, foodstuffs, molasses, and rum that were brought into the colonies. Shortly afterward, the Stamp Act was introduced by the British, requiring the purchase of revenue stamps on all imports.

Two years after the Declaration of Independence was signed, the colonies joined together by a formal agreement known as the Articles of Confederation. Although the colonies called themselves the United States of America, they remained a union of independent states. The central government had no power to levy taxes and could only request the states to contribute monies in proportion to assessed value of their respective lands. Each state had its own tariff laws and resorted to stringent measures against each other, manifested for selfish reasons as a protective measure or for reprisal.

Despite the conflicts between the colonies, the people realized that a unification of the states was necessary for survival, which led to the Constitutional Convention of 1787. The Constitution was drafted and sent to Congress and became effective March 4, 1789. Some of the states desired heavy duties as a protective measure against European competition and others favored free trade.

On July 31, 1787, the U.S. Customs Service was created at a crucial time in the annals of the thirteen colonies. It was organized to overcome the collapse of the new government through the collection of duties on imports and eventually led to its solidarity. The thirteen states resolved that a uniform tariff would be very expedient. (Sec. 8 Article 1 of the Constitution provides: "Congress shall have the power to levy and collect taxes, duties, imports and excises.") According to statistics, this was realized and the collection of duty for its first year was slightly more than two million dollars, as compared to statistical reports for 1973 in the sum of about four billion one hundred million dollars.

Chapter 2

ESSENTIALS FOR TRAVELING ABROAD

Proof of United States Citizenship

United States passports are not required for travel by citizens to any territory subject to the jurisdiction of the United States including the Canal Zone. Certain foreign countries do not require one for short visits. However, one should be fortified with a passport to facilitate reentry into the U.S.A.

A native-born citizen should have in his possession his birth or baptismal certificate, or some other personal document to establish his citizenship, or an affidavit of his birth executed by his parents, or some other person having personal knowledge of the date and place of his birth.

A naturalized citizen should carry his naturalization certificate. Persons born abroad may carry an approved certificate of birth by the Department of State. When citizenship was acquired through birth abroad to parents of U.S. citizenship, a Consular Report of Birth, issued by the Department of State, should be submitted.

Passport agencies are located in the following cities: Boston, Chicago, Honolulu, Los Angeles, Miami, New Orleans, New York, Philadelphia, San Francisco, Seattle, and Washington, D.C.

Visas

A visa is the permission granted by a foreign government to an alien to enter and remain in that country for a certain period of time. To obtain a visa you must relinquish your passport with completed visa application forms to the consular official in the United States of the country requiring the visa. It takes one to several weeks for approval and then it is entered in the passport.

Eastern European countries require that U.S. citizens obtain a visa before entering their countries. Western European countries do not require visas for U.S. citizens staying up to three months. While Central and South American countries do not require visas, a tourist card or entry permit is often required and may be obtained from a travel agency or airline serving these countries.

Immunization

Under the International Health Regulations adopted by the World Health Organization, an International Certification of Vaccination against smallpox, cholera, and yellow fever may be required as a condition of entry to any country. For return to the United States, only a smallpox certificate will be required if within the past fourteen days a traveler has visited a country reporting smallpox. Specific information on required immunization for travel to all areas of the world may be obtained from your local or state health department.

Currency

Some foreign countries require the traveler to declare the amount of money brought into their country and the amount of money taken out. There are limitations that should be checked with the respective consul general of the country that you intend to visit.

It is a good idea to ascertain the conversion of United States money to the equivalent in foreign currency. This information can be obtained at any bank that handles foreign exchange.

Registration of Valuable Effects Prior to Travel Abroad

Foreign-made personal articles to be taken abroad, such as watches, binoculars, cameras, or jewelry, should be registered with customs before departure at the airport or at the custom house. Request a duplicate copy of your registration from customs and present it on reentry into the United States (Customs Form 4457).

All foreign-made articles are subject to duty each time they are imported unless they are registered with customs before leaving the country. Your duplicate copy on reentry will facilitate matters.

Domestic articles taken abroad, if not identifiable with a marking to indicate country of origin, should also be registered with customs. If you fail to register these articles, and in order to overcome any obstacle of uncertainty, you should have proof, such as a bill of sale, showing that these articles were purchased in the United States.

Chapter 3

RATES OF DUTY APPLICABLE TO PURCHASES ABROAD

Customs duties are classified as ad valorem, specific, or compound. An ad valorem rate is a percentage that is applied to the dutiable value of the imported article. For example: Dutiable value $140, rate of duty 10% = $14 duty.

A specific duty is a specified amount depending upon weight. For example: Dutiable value of $140, net weight of the imported articles 7 pounds, rate of duty 15¢ per pound-- duty would be 7 pounds x 15¢ per pound = $1.05.

A compound duty combines specific and ad valorem duties based on an article. For example:

Dutiable value $140, net weight of article 12 pounds
@ 15¢ per pound, plus 10% ad valorem

Duty would be 12 lbs. x 15¢/lb. = $ 1.80
$140 @ 10%   =   14.00
$15.80

Articles that are imported will be appraised on their wholesale value. The list shown on the following pages consists of items chiefly imported by tourists and travelers. It should be noted that the customs duties are higher for articles produced in Communist countries (except for Poland, Rumania, and Yugoslavia, which receive the benefit of the regular rates of duty).

All rates shown are subject to change. (See Appendix.)

ALCOHOLIC BEVERAGES

Article	Internal Revenue Tax	Customs Duty	Customs Duty Communist Countries
Beer	$ 9.00 bbl. (31 gal.)	$ .06 per gal.	$ .50/gal.
Brandy	$10.50*	$ .50 to $1.25 gal.	$5.00*
Gin	$10.50*	$ .50*	$5.00*
Liqueurs	$10.50*	$ .50*	$5.00*
Rum	$10.50*	$1.75*	$5.00*
Whisky			
Scotch	$10.50*	$ .51*	$5.00*
Irish	$10.50*	$ .51*	$5.00*
Other	$10.50*	$ .62*	$5.00*
Wine			
Sparkling (Champagne)	$ 2.40 to $3.40	$1.17	$6.00*
Still	$ .17 to $2.25	$ .315 to $1.00	$1.25*

*Per United States gallon (128 fluid ounces) if under 100 proof. Duty and tax are based on proof gallon if 100 proof or over.

Article	Customs Duty (Most Favored Nations)	Customs Duty Communist Countries
Antiques - produced prior to 100 years before the date of entry (obtain proof of antiquity from seller)	Free	Free
Automobiles - passenger	3%	10%
Bags - Hand, leather	8-1/2% to 10%	35%
Beads - Imitation precious and semiprecious stones	7% to 13%	40% to 75%
Ivory	10%	45%
Binoculars - prism	20%	60%
Opera and field glasses	8-1/2%	45%
Books - English or foreign language (textual matter)	Free	Free
Cameras - Motion picture, over $50 each	6%	20%
Still, over $10 each	7-1/2%	20%
Cases, leather	8-1/2% to 10%	35%

Article	Customs Duty (Most Favored Nations)	Customs Duty Communist Countries
Cameras (cont.)		
Lenses	12-1/2%	45%
Candy - Confectionery and other confectionery not specially provided for	7%	40%
Chess Sets	10%	50%
China - Bone	17-1/2%	$.10/dz. pcs. + 70%
Nonbone, other than tableware	22-1/2%	70%
China Tableware - nonbone, available in 77-pc. sets		
Valued not over $10 per set	$.10/dz. pcs. + 48%	$.10/dz. pcs. + 70%
Valued over $10 but not over $24 per set	$.10/dz. pcs. + 55%	$.10/dz. pcs. + 70%
Valued over $24 but not over $56 per set	$.10/dz. pcs. + 36%	$.10/dz. pcs. + 70%
Valued over $56 per set	$.05/dz. pcs. + 18%	$.10/dz. pcs. + 70%
Cigarette Lighters - Pocket, valued at over $5 per dz. pcs.	22-1/2%	110%
Table lighters	12%	60%

Article	Customs Duty (Most Favored Nations)	Customs Duty Communist Countries
Clocks - Valued at over $5 but not over $10 each	$.75 + 16% + $.0625 for each jewel	Obtain information from import specialist at custom house or airport
Valued over $10 each	$1.12 ea. + 16% + $.0625 for each jewel	
Dolls and Parts	17-1/2%	70%
Drawings - (Works of Art)		
Original	Free	Free
Copies, done entirely by hand	Free	Free
Earthenware Tableware - available in 77-pc. sets		
Valued not over $3.30/set	$.05/dz. pcs. + 14%	$.10/dz. pcs. + 50%
Valued over $3.30/set but not over $7.00/set	$.10/dz. pcs. + 21%	$.10/dz. pcs. + 50%
Valued over $7/set but not over $12/set	$.10/dz. pcs. + 21%	$.10/dz. pcs. + 50%
Valued over $12/set	$.05/dz. pcs. + 10-1/2%	$.10/dz. pcs. + 50%
Figurines - China Bone	12-1/2%	70%

Article	Customs Duty (Most Favored Nations)	Customs Duty Communist Countries
Figurines - China (cont.)		
Nonbone chinaware	22-1/2%	70%
Film - Exposed motion-picture film in any form on which pictures or sound and pictures have been recorded, developed or not developed	48/100ths of a cent per linear foot	3¢ per linear foot
Other exposed or exposed and developed film would be classifiable as photographs	4% of their value	25%
Flowers - Artificial, plastic	21%	60%
Fruit - Prepared, preserved	35%	35%
Fur - Wearing apparel	8-1/2% to 18-1/2%	35% to 50%
Other manufactures of	8-1/2% to 18-1/2%	35% to 50%
Furniture - Wood, chairs	8-1/2%	40%
Wood, other than chairs	5%	40%
Glass - Tableware	20% to 50%	60%

Article	Customs Duty (Most Favored Nations)	Customs Duty Communist Countries
Gloves - Not lace or net, plain vegetable fibers, woven	25%	25%
Wool, over $4 per dozen	$.375/lb. + 18-1/2%	$.50/lb. + 50%
Fur	10%	50%
Horsehide or cowhide	15%	25%
Golf Balls	6%	30%
Handkerchiefs - Cotton, hand embroidered	$.04 ea. + 40%	$.04 ea. + 40%
Cotton, plain	25%	37%
Other vegetable fiber, plain	9%	50%
Ivory - Manufactures of	6%	35%
Jade - Cut, but not set and suitable for use in the manufacture of jewelry	2-1/2%	10%
Other articles of jade	21%	50%
Jewelry - Precious metal or stone Silver chief value, valued not over $18/dz. pcs.	27-1/2%	110%
Other	12%	80%

Article	Customs Duty (Most Favored Nations)	Customs Duty Communist Countries
Leather - Pocketbooks, bags	8-1/2% to 10%	35%
Other manufactures of	4% to 14%	35%
Mah Jong Sets	10%	50%
Motorcycles	5%	10%
Mushrooms - Dried	$.032/lb. + 10%	$.10/lb. + 45%
Musical Instruments - Music boxes, wood	8%	40%
Woodwind, except bagpipes	7-1/2%	40%
Bagpipes	Free	40%
Paintings - Works of Art)		
Original	Free	Free
Copies, done entirely by hand	Free	Free
Pearls - Loose or temporarily strung and without clasp		
Genuine	Free	10%
Cultured	2-1/2%	10%

Article	Customs Duty (Most Favored Nations)	Customs Duty Communist Countries
Pearls (cont.)		
Imitation	20%	60%
Perfume - Cologne, Toilet Water		
Not containing alcohol	7-1/2%	75%
Containing alcohol	$.08/lb. + 7-1/2%	$.40/lb. + 75%
Postage Stamps	Free	Free
Radios - Transistors	10-2/5%	35%
Others	6%	35%
Records - Phonograph	5%	30%
Shavers - Electric	6-1/2%	35%
Shoes - Leather	2-1/2% to 20%	10% to 30%
Skis and Ski Equipment		
Ski Boots (mostly plastic)	Free to 20%	20% to 35%
Ski and Snow Shoes	8%	33-1/3%

Article	Customs Duty (Most Favored Nations)	Customs Duty Communist Countries
Skis and Ski Equipment (cont.)		
Toboggans	5%	33-1/3%
Other	9%	45%
Slippers - Leather	5%	20%
Stones - Cut but not set		
Diamonds not over one-half carat	4%	10%
Diamonds over one-half carat	5%	10%
Sweaters - Wool		
Valued over $18 per lb. wholly of cashmere	$.375/lb. + 15.5%	$.50/lb. + 50%
Other	$.375/lb. + 20%	$.50/lb. + 50%
Tableware and Flatware		
Knives, forks, flatware:		
Silver handles	$.04 ea. + 8-1/2%	$.16 ea. + 45%
Stainless steel	$.01 ea. + 12-1/2%	$.02 ea. + 45%
Spoons and tableware:		
Silver handles	12-1/2%	65%
Stainless steel	17%	40%

Article	Customs Duty (Most Favored Nations)	Customs Duty Communist Countries
Tape Recorders	5-1/2% to 7-1/2%	35%
Toilet Preparations		
Not containing alcohol	7-1/2%	75%
Containing alcohol	$.08/lb. + 7-1/2%	$.40/lb. + 75%
Toys - Having a spring mechanism	22%	70%
Others	17-1/2%	70%
Vegetables - Prepared	17-1/2%	35%
Watches	Obtain information from import specialist at custom house or airport	
Wearing Apparel		
Embroidered or ornamented	21% to 42-1/2%	Obtain information from import specialist at custom house or airport
Not embroidered, not ornamented:		
cotton knit	21%	"
cotton, not knit	8% to 21%	"
linen, not knit	7-1/2%	
manmade fiber, knit	$.25/lb. + 32-1/2%	

19

Article	Customs Duty (Most Favored Nations)	Customs Duty Communist Countries
Wearing Apparel (cont.)		
Not embroidered, not ornamented:		
manmade fiber, not knit	$.25/lb. + 27-1/2%	Obtain information from import specialist at custom house or airport
silk, knit	10%	"
silk, not knit	16%	
wool, knit	$.375/lb. + 15-1/2% to 32%	
wool, not knit	$.25 to $.375/lb. + 21%	
Wood		
Carvings	8%	33-1/3%
Manufactures of	8%	33-1/3%

20

Chapter 4

RESIDENCE STATUS OF ARRIVING PERSONS

Residents

Citizens of the United States or persons who have formerly resided in the United States shall be deemed residents returning from abroad (if they left the United States for traveling, working, or studying abroad) unless it can be proven that they have established a home outside of the United States.

Nonresidents

Any person arriving in the United States who is not a resident of the United States or who, though a resident of the United States, is not returning from abroad, shall be treated as a nonresident.

Optional claim of nonresident status

A returning resident arriving in the United States may claim at his option the status of a nonresident if he intends to remain in the United States for only a short period of time before returning abroad, providing it is allowed by customs in compliance with its rules and regulations.

Declarations are required for all articles brought into the United States by an individual and shall be declared to a customs officer at the port of first arrival in the United States, on a conveyance enroute to the United States on which a customs officer is assigned for that purpose, or at a preclearance office in a foreign country where a United States customs officer is stationed for that purpose.

All articles acquired abroad and in your possession at the time of your return must be declared. For example, articles such as wedding and birthday presents; items you have been requested to bring home for another person; articles you import that you intend to sell or use in your business; repairs or alterations made to any articles taken abroad and returned, whether or not there were any fees for such repair or alteration.

The price actually paid for each article must be stated on your declaration whether it be in United States currency or its equivalent in the country where purchased.

Declarations

Written declarations by returning residents are required for the following:

1. Individual items not exceeding $5.00 per item, which represents the fair retail value in the country of acquisition, may be grouped on the written declaration as "miscellaneous," however, not to exceed $50.00.

2. Effects of a returning resident are entitled to free entry under Item #810.20 of the Tariff Schedules of the United States, which provides: professional books, implements, instruments, tools of trade in one's occupation or employment that have been taken abroad by him or for his account. If any of these articles is imported as baggage but not passed under a baggage declaration, and as an unaccompanied shipment by the passenger, shall be entered in the same manner as a cargo importation.

3. Automobiles or other vehicles of a returning resident from countries other than Canada or Mexico require that the cost of all repairs or alterations, if any, to the articles taken abroad must be itemized.

4. Articles imported by or for the account of any person arriving in the United States from a foreign country.

5. Books, libraries, furniture and similar household effects, if actually used abroad by him or his family, for not less than one year, and not intended for any other person, or for sale, are free of duty.

Written declarations--nonresidents. Effects of a nonresident are entitled to free entry under Item #812.10 of the Tariff Schedules of the United States, which provides: Wearing apparel, articles of personal adornment, e.g., watches, jewelry, toilet articles and similar personal effects, all the foregoing if actually owned by and in the possession of such person abroad at the time of or prior to his departure for the United States and if appropriate for his own personal use and intended only for such use and not for any other person and not for sale.

Oral declarations by residents are permitted under the following circumstances:

1. A returning resident may make an oral declaration of his purchases if they did not exceed his duty-free exemption.

2. Personal or household effects taken out of this country and brought back, if the cost or value of alterations and dutiable repairs made abroad does not exceed $100, or $200 in case of repairs or alterations made in Samoa, Guam, or Virgin Islands, and if not more than $100 shall have been acquired elsewhere than in such insular possessions.

3. None of his accompanying articles are forwarded in bond.

4. None of his accompanying articles are imported for the account of any other person or for sale.

Oral declarations--nonresidents. An arriving nonresident may make an oral declaration if the articles he has declared are covered by his personal exemption.

Family declarations. A family group residing in one household, traveling together and having the same residence status, may be permitted to declare orally articles acquired abroad for the personal or household use of any member of the family if the value of such articles does not exceed the total amount of the exemption to which the family group is entitled, e.g., a family of four may bring in articles valued up to $400 retail on one declaration even if the articles acquired by one member exceeds his $100 exemption.

Where a written declaration is required, one member of a family group may declare for all. Servants accompanying a family group shall not be included in the family declaration.

Accompanying Articles

Generally articles shall be considered as accompanying a passenger or brought in by him if the articles arrive on the same vessel, vehicle, or aircraft on the same date as that of his arrival in the United States.

Baggage shipped as freight. Articles in baggage shipped as freight on a bill of lading or airway bill shall be considered as accompanying a passenger when the baggage arrives on the conveyance on which he or she arrives in the United States.

Precleared articles. Articles in baggage, or in baggage shipped as freight, shall be considered as accompanying a passenger if examined at an established preclearance station and the baggage is hand-carried, checked, or manifested on the conveyance on which he arrives in the United States.

23

Automobiles. An automobile that arrives on the same mode of conveyance on the same date that a passenger arrives in the United States shall be considered as accompanying him.

Misdirected baggage. Baggage that arrives on the same mode of conveyance ahead of or after a passenger shall be treated as accompanying him if it is fully evident to the examining officer from the circumstances that:

1. The passenger intended the baggage to arrive with him; and

2. It was misdirected through no fault of the passenger.

Articles acquired abroad that do not accompany the passenger or on his return cannot be included in his customs exemption. All merchandise imported into the United States is subject to payment of customs duty unless it has been specifically exempted by law.

Articles imported in excess of your customs exemption will be subject to duty calculated by the customs inspector, unless the items are entitled to free entry or are prohibited. He will place the items having the highest rate of duty under your exemption and any items that are dutiable upon the lower rate; for example: if the total appraised value of the imported articles is $250 and the rates applicable are 15% and 6% ad valorem, the customs inspector will apply the 15% rate of duty to the $100 exemption and 6% to the $150 balance.

The passenger must state the fair retail value of the articles purchased and it is advisable to keep the sales slips of all purchases made abroad. Customs officers will make all allowance permitted from the retail values.

Trade-mark violations. Such articles arriving as accompanying baggage, or on the passenger's person, may be exported or destroyed under customs supervision at the request of the passenger, or may be released if he removes or obliterates the marks in the manner acceptable to the customs inspector at the time of the examination of the articles.

Payment of duty. At the time of passenger's arrival, payment of duty must be made in:

1. United States currency; or

2. Personal check in the amount of duty drawn on a national or state bank or trust company in the United States, made payable to the "U.S. Customs Service."

3. Government checks, money orders, or travelers checks are acceptable if they do not exceed the amount of the duty by more than $50.

24

4. Second endorsements are not acceptable.

5. Identification must be presented, e.g., traveler's passport or Social Security card, etc.

Entry of Unaccompanied Shipments of Effects Subject to
Personal Exemptions

Declaration to support free entry. When effects claimed to be free of duty do not accompany the person on his arrival in the United States or are forwarded in bond, a declaration of the person on Customs Form 3299 shall be required to support the claim for free entry. However, an oral declaration may be accepted in lieu of a written declaration on Customs Form 3299, for the effects of a resident that are free of duty. Effects of returning residents are entitled to free entry (except automobiles and other vehicles of residents returning from countries other than Canada or Mexico) and need not be itemized if a written declaration is required.

Articles imported by or for the account of any person arriving in the United States who is not a returning resident, such as: 1. Wearing apparel, articles of personal adornment, toilet articles, and similar personal effects; all the foregoing, if actually owned by and in the possession of such person abroad at the time of or prior to his departure for the United States, and if appropriate for his own personal use and intended only for such use and not for any other person nor for sale, are free of duty.

2. Automobiles, trailers, aircraft, motorcycles, bicycles, baby carriages, boats, horse-drawn conveyances, horses, and similar means of transportation, and the usual equipment accompanying the foregoing; any of the foregoing imported in connection with the arrival of such person and to be used in the United States only for the transportation of such person, his family, and guests, and such incidental carriage of articles as may be appropriate to his personal use of the conveyance, are free of duty.

Exemption from entry. If the U.S. customs district director is satisfied that an entry would serve no good purpose, none need be required, but evidence of ownership for customs purposes, such as a carrier's certificate or properly endorsed bill of lading, shall be required with the declaration. Such exemption from entry may also be applied with respect to household effects or tools of trade entitled to free entry that are unaccompanied or forwarded in bond.

Unclaimed baggage. Articles in passengers' baggage on which duties due are not paid and baggage not claimed within a reasonable time shall be treated as unclaimed and sent to General Order (a designated bonded warehouse where the merchandise is kept) at the risk and expense of the consignee or owner of the merchandise. If all the charges are not paid and the merchandise is still unclaimed during a period of one year, it will be sold at public auction. It is required that the owner of such baggage be notified. The basic purpose for the sale is that the government should realize the duty, if any, and the other charges. During this period the charges for transportation and storage accumulate.

Failure to declare. Any article in a passenger's baggage arriving from a foreign country that is not declared is subject to seizure at the time the violation was detected and the personal penalty prescribed in Title 19 United States Code Annotated 1497 shall be demanded from the passenger, and he shall be liable to a penalty equal to the value of the article. If the article is not seized, a claim for personal penalty shall be made against the person who imported the article. No duty shall be collected since undeclared articles are treated as smuggled.

There could be a remission of penalty, if it could be satisfactorily established that the article would have been free of duty and Internal Revenue tax if it had been properly declared, or its importation is not prohibited or restricted or the failure to declare was not due to willful negligence or fraudulent intent.

False or Fraudulent Statement

A passenger who makes any false or fraudulent statement to a customs inspector who may thereby release any article free of duty or on the payment of less than the proper amount of duty, shall be deemed to be in violation of Sec. 592 of the Tariff Act of 1930 and Title 19 United States Code Annotated 1592. If the discovery is made then the article will be subject to seizure, or if the article is not available for seizure, then the appraised value will be the domestic value of the article at the time and place of appraisement.

"Duty Free" Shops

Articles bought in "duty free" shops in foreign countries are subject to U.S. Customs exemptions and restrictions.

Articles purchased in United States "duty free" shops are subject to U.S. Customs duty if one reenters the United States, e.g., liquor bought in a "duty free' shop before entering Canada and brought back into the United States will be subject to duty and Internal Revenue tax.

Chapter 5

EXEMPTIONS

Residents

Articles acquired abroad. Each returning resident is entitled to bring in free of duty, including Internal Revenue tax, articles for his personal or household use that were purchased or acquired abroad as an incident of the foreign journey from which he is returning and accompanying him on his arrival. The aggregate fair retail value in the country of purchase of such articles shall not exceed $100 except that in the case of a resident arriving directly or indirectly from American Samoa, Guam, or the Virgin Islands of the United States, of which not more than $100 shall have been acquired elsewhere, the exemption shall be $200.

Gifts. An article acquired abroad by a returning resident and imported by him to be disposed of after importation as his bona fide gift is considered to be for personal use of the returning resident and may be included in his exemption.

Tobacco products. No more than 100 cigars may be included. There is no limitation of cigarettes and tobacco for one's personal use.

Alcoholic beverages. No alcoholic beverages shall be included in the case of an individual who has not attained the age of twenty-one.

No more than one quart of alcoholic beverages may be included in the exemption, unless the individual is arriving directly or indirectly from American Samoa, Guam, or the Virgin Islands, in which case he shall be entitled to not more than one wine gallon.

United States postal laws prohibit the shipment of alcoholic beverages by mail.

Exemption not applicable. If articles are intended for sale or commission for account of another person with or without compensation for services rendered, they are subject to the payment of duty. Articles acquired on one journey and left in a foreign country cannot be allowed the exemption accruing upon the return of the resident from a subsequent journey.

A returning resident who has received a total exemption of less than $100 under the $100 exemption, or less than $200 under the $200 exemption in connection with his return from one journey is not entitled to apply the remainder of either amount to articles acquired abroad on a subsequent journey.

Length of stay for exemption of articles acquired abroad. The $100 exemption for articles acquired abroad shall not be allowed unless the returning resident has remained beyond the territorial limits of the United States for not less than forty-eight hours, except a resident arriving directly in the United States from Mexico.

The exemption may be allowed on articles acquired abroad by a returning resident arriving directly from Mexico without regard to the length of time the person has remained outside the territorial limits of the United States.

The $200 exemption applicable in the case of the arrival of a resident returning directly or indirectly from the Virgin Islands of the United States may be allowed without regard to the length of time such person has remained outside the territorial limits of the United States.

Frequency of allowance of exemptions of articles acquired abroad--a thirty-day period shall not be granted to a returning resident who has taken advantage of such exemption within the thirty-day period immediately preceding his return to the United States.

An article furnished by a foreign supplier to replace a like article previously exempted from duty under the $100 or $200 exemptions acquired abroad and found to be unsatisfactory, shall be returned to customs custody and exported under customs supervision at the expense of the importer within sixty days after importation and a certificate of registration on Customs Form 4455 shall be issued to the importer with instructions as to its use.

A declared article found damaged upon examination to the extent that it is so badly damaged that it is unusable would constitute a nonimportation. In such case, Customs Form 4455 shall be issued to the importer, and duplicate replacement shall be allowed entry as having been acquired abroad, provided no charge is made to the importer for the duplicate replacement.

Residents--effects taken abroad. Automobiles and other vehicles, aircraft, and boats, together with their accessories, may be brought in free of duty if taken abroad for noncommercial use. Household and personal effects taken out of the United States and returned are free of duty.

In the case of repair or alteration of personal or household effects taken abroad that have been advanced in value or improved in condition while abroad by repairs or by alterations, which did not change the identity of the articles, the cost of value of the repairs or alterations is subject to duty unless all or part of such cost is covered by the $100 or $200 exemption for articles acquired abroad.

A personal or household effect taken abroad and there changed into a different article is dutiable at the full value unless there is a provision for free entry.

Nonresidents

Personal effects. A nonresident arriving in the United States, regardless of age, is entitled to enter free of duty and Internal Revenue tax his wearing apparel, articles of personal adornment, toilet articles, and personal effects for the use of the nonresident while traveling, e.g., hunting and fishing equipment, wheelchairs for invalids, pet and hunting dogs.

For personal use--tobacco products. No more than 50 cigars, 300 cigarettes, and 3 pounds of smoking tobacco may be included.

Alcoholic beverages. No more than one quart of alcoholic beverages brought in by an adult nonresident for his personal use may be included.

Gifts. A nonresident who is allowed a $100 gift exemption may include no more than one gallon of alcoholic beverages and no more than 100 cigars under such exemption of duty and Internal Revenue tax, provided the articles accompanying him are to be disposed of only as bona fide gifts.

Frequency of allowance. The exemption for gifts may be allowed only if the nonresident has not claimed the exemptions within the immediately preceding six months, and he intends to remain in the United States for not less than seventy-two hours.

Nonresidents--vehicles and other conveyances. Nonresidents are entitled to free entry and Internal Revenue tax for autos, trailers, aircraft, motorcycles, baby carriages, boats, and similar means of transportation, if such articles are imported in connection with the arrival of the nonresident, his family and guests and such incidental carriage of articles as may be appropriate to his personal use of the conveyance.

Such articles if sold must be reported to the nearest customs district director and customs duty paid.

Examples for household effects used abroad. Furniture, carpets, paintings, tableware, books, libraries, household furnishings, and effects actually used abroad for not less than one year by residents or nonresidents and not intended for any other person or for sale may be allowed entry free of duty and tax. Household effects used abroad not less than one year during the period of use may be allowed free of duty whether or not the importer owned the effects at the time of such use. The year of use need not be continuous. The owner claiming free of duty should submit Customs Form 3299.

Arrival of effects more than ten years after arrival of importer from the country in which the effects were used shall not be admitted free of duty under this exemption unless the district director is satisfied with the importer's explanation that the effects were unavoidably detained beyond the ten-year period.

Exemptions for Effects of Citizens Dying Abroad

Articles claimed to be personal and household effects, the title of which is in the estate of a citizen of the United States who died abroad, may be allowed entry free of duty and tax.

If the value of such effects does not exceed $250 entry may be permitted.

The district director shall require in connection with the entry the written statement of a person having knowledge of the facts or shall otherwise satisfy himself as to the citizenship of the deceased owner of the effects at the time of death.

Special Exemption for Personal or Household Articles

For a returning resident who is not entitled to the $100 or $200 exemption for articles acquired abroad and a nonresident arriving in the United States who is not entitled to an exemption for gifts, the following exemptions shall apply: When the aggregate fair retail value of all articles not otherwise entitled to an exemption does not exceed ten dollars, the exemption would apply where personal or household articles, such as groceries or clothes, accompany a person who lives in border cities and travels in neighboring foreign cities. This exemption shall not be applied to articles subject to Internal Revenue tax other than cigarettes not in excess of fifty, cigars not in excess of ten, alcoholic beverages not in excess of four pounds or alcoholic perfumery not in excess of four ounces. Family grouping of exemption is not allowed.

Chapter 6

EXAMINATION OF BAGGAGE

Opening of Baggage, Compartments or Vehicles

In general it is required that all passengers shall open their trunk, traveling bag, valise, vehicles, or locked compartments of baggage for the purpose of examination. However, upon refusal, they shall be detained and shall be treated as unclaimed.

On arrival from Canada or Mexico. If the owner or agent of any baggage or vehicle arriving from Canada or Mexico refuses to open it, and if any articles are subject to duty, or if the container is found upon opening by a customs officer to contain prohibited merchandise, the whole contents of the container or vehicle shall be subject to forfeiture.

Examination of Air Travelers' Baggage in Foreign Territory

Examination and surrender of declaration. The baggage of persons traveling by air may be examined and passed at places in foreign territory where United States customs offices have been established for that purpose. When baggage is examined in foreign territory, the baggage declaration shall be surrendered to the customs officer at the airport of departure for the United States prior to boarding the flight.

Subsequently acquired articles. When a person whose baggage has been examined and passed in foreign territory as described above subsequently acquires additional articles prior to return to the United States, the customs officer to whom the declaration was surrendered may permit the amendment of that declaration to include the additional articles.

Articles Subject to Duty

The inspector who examines the baggage of any person arriving in the United States may examine, determine the dutiable value of, collect duty on, and pass articles accompanying the arriving person that are for his personal or household use but are subject to duty, including articles imported to be disposed of by him as bona fide gifts.

Articles Not for Personal Use

   Valued at not more than $250. The inspector may also examine, determine the dutiable value of, collect duty on, and pass articles accompanying any person arriving in the United States that are properly listed on the baggage declaration that are not for the personal or household use of the declarant, or that are intended for sale, or are brought in on commission for another, provided the aggregate value of such articles is not more than $250.
   Valued over $250 but not over $500. Articles in the baggage of or otherwise accompanying any person arriving in the United States that have an aggregate value over $250 but not over $500 and are not intended for his personal or household use, or are intended for sale or are brought in on commission for another, may be examined and entered and cleared on a baggage declaration at the place of their arrival with a passenger if:
   (a) The articles are accompanied by a proper invoice if one is required; and
   (b) It is practicable to appraise the articles at the place of arrival.

Determination of Dutiable Value

   Principles applied. In determining the dutiable value of articles examined, the inspector shall apply the principles of Section 402 or Section 402a of the Tariff Act of 1930, as amended, and shall not regard the declared value or price as conclusive.
   Adjustment of value declared. An adjustment shall be made by the inspector whenever the purchase price or value declared differs from the fair retail value, whether by reason of depreciation due to wear or use, circumstances of purchase or acquisition, or for any other reason. He shall give due consideration to the condition of the articles at the time of importation, but he shall not make any allowance for wear and use in excess of 25 per cent of the declared price or value of a worn or used article. A passenger who desires to claim a larger allowance may arrange for formal entry and appraisement of his goods.

Reexamination and Protest

Reexamination. Should the customs officer question the declared value, he may order any or all of a passenger's baggage to the public stores (customhouse) for reexamination. Passengers dissatisfied with the assessment of duty on their baggage may demand a reexamination, provided the articles have not been removed from customs custody. In either case, a receipt for the baggage to be examined or reexamined shall be given on Customs Form 6051.

Protest. If the passenger remains dissatisfied with the assessment of duty after reexamination, he shall pay the duty assessed and may protest the decision of the district director to the regional commissioner of the port of entry. Note: The district director is known as the area director at the port of New York (Region II).

Chapter 7

IMPORTATIONS AND EXPORTATIONS BY MAIL

Importations

Shipping by mail has its advantages both to the tourist and the importer of merchandise if the value is under $250. If the package is delivered by the post office before the tourist returns home, and if the parcel is dutiable, someone from the family can pay the duty to the postman or can accept the parcel if there is no duty charge.

Another advantage for shipping by mail from abroad is to minimize the cost of shipping and brokerage charges. Should the seller of the articles send the parcels by freight, whether sea or air, the services of a broker may be required.

Where parcels are sent by mail, a customs declaration must accompany each shipment. It must give an accurate description and value of the contents and be securely attached to the parcel, or if several parcels, the address side should state "invoice enclosed."

Shipments without declarations and invoices that are not accompanied by a customs declaration and invoice may be subject to seizure and forfeiture particularly if found to contain material prohibited or contrary to law.

If a mail shipment exceeds $250, the addressee is notified to prepare and file a formal customs entry (consumption entry) at the customs port nearest him.

If the total value does not exceed $500, a commercial invoice is required with the entry. If the value exceeds $500, a special customs invoice must be furnished when the merchandise is dutiable; it does not apply generally to unconditionally free merchandise.

The U.S. Postal Service sends all incoming mail shipments to the U.S. Customs Service for examination. Packages valued under $250 that are free of duty are returned to the post office for delivery to the addressee without additional postage, handling charges, or other fees. For packages containing dutiable articles valued under $250, customs will attach a mail entry showing the amount of duty to be paid by the addressee plus a postal fee (in addition to the prepaid postage) authorized by the International Postal Convention agreements as postal reimbursement to the postal service for its work in clearing packages through customs and delivering them; it will then return them to the post office. If the addressee has arranged to pick up such a shipment at the customs office where it is being processed, the customs officer will prepare an informal entry and the postal service at that office will collect the duty.

If there are separate shipments of merchandise mailed at different times as shown by declarations, they shall not be combined for the purpose of requiring a formal entry even though they reach customs at the same time and are carried by a single order or contract in excess of $250, unless there was a splitting of the shipment for the purpose of avoiding making an entry or the payment of duty.

Packages other than parcel post--letter-class mail and other mail--such as commercial papers, printed matter, and samples of merchandise, must bear on the addressee side a label, <u>Form C1</u> provided for the Universal Postal Union, or the endorsement "may be opened for customs purposes before delivery." Parcels not so labeled or endorsed and found to contain merchandise subject to duty or tax are subject to forfeiture.

The district director of customs will pass free of duty and tax, without issuing an entry, on packages containing merchandise having an aggregate fair retail value of not over one dollar.

Free entry will apply to packages containing bona fide gifts from a person in a foreign country to a person in the United States having an aggregate fair retail value in the country of exportation not exceeding ten dollars.

If bona fide gifts are sent from Guam or the Virgin Islands, and if the aggregate fair retail value does not exceed twenty dollars, it will be allowed free of duty.

<u>Marking requirements as to the country of origin.</u> If for the personal use of the importer or tourist and not intended for sale in its imported condition, it need not be marked.

<u>Trade-mark violations.</u> Articles arriving by mail valued at $250 or less may be exported or destroyed at the request of the addressee or may be released if he removes or obliterates the marks in a manner acceptable to the customs officer.

<u>Mail entries--undeliverable packages.</u> If for any reason

an undeliverable package, known or supposed to be dutiable, is not returned to the country of origin and forwarded to another country in accordance with the postal regulations, it will be delivered to customs for disposition under customs rules and regulations governing seized or unclaimed merchandise.

Shipment of alcoholic beverages to the United States is prohibited.

Procedures for obtaining administrative review. If an addressee is dissatisfied with the amount of duty assessed under a mail entry, he may obtain administrative review in the following ways:

(a) He may pay the assessed duty, take delivery of the merchandise, and send a copy of the mail entry to the issuing customs office indicated on the mail entry, together with a statement of the reason it is believed the duty assessed is incorrect. Any invoices, bills of sale, or other evidence should be submitted with the statement. The addressee should show the mail entry number and date on his statement instead of sending a copy of the mail entry, but this may result in delay since a copy of the entry will have to be obtained from the regional commissioner of customs, at the port of entry, before the entry can be amended.

(b) He may postpone acceptance of the shipment, and within the time allowed by the postal regulations, provide the postmaster with a written statement of his objections. The postmaster will forward the mail entry together with the addressee's statement and any invoices, bills of sale, or other evidence submitted by the addressee, to the district director who issued the entry and retain custody of the shipment until advice is received from the district director as to the disposition to be made.

(c) He may pay the assessed duty and take delivery of the merchandise, and file a protest.

Requests for adjustment in the amount of duty assessed under mail entries shall be made in such time that the request can be acted upon by the district director within ninety days after receipt of the package and payment of the duties by the addressee. Protests must be filed not later than ninety days after payment of the duties by the addressee.

Amendment of entry. If the district director is satisfied that the objection is valid and timely, he shall amend the mail entry. If the duty has already been paid, the regional commissioner shall issue an appropriate refund of duty.

If the district director believes the duty originally assessed was correct, he shall send the addressee a notice in
writing that the request for refund of duty has been denied.
If the duty has not been paid, the mail entry shall be returned
to the postmaster concerned, together with a copy of the notice
sent to the addressee. The postmaster will then collect the
duty and deliver the shipment, or, if the addressee refuses to
pay the duty, will treat the shipment as undeliverable.

Rates of duty not binding. Rates of duty assessed on a
mail entry, whether assessed on the original entry or as
amendments, are not binding for future importations. A binding ruling on tariff classification may be obtained by writing
to Headquarters, U. S. Customs, Washington, D. C., and requesting a binding ruling. A full description of the merchandise must accompany the request including, where possible,
a sample of the merchandise.

Exportations

Shipments from continuous government custody. Merchandise imported into the United States, unless nonmailable,
may be exported by any class of mail without the payment of
duties if:

(a) The merchandise has remained continuously in the
custody of the government (customs or postal authorities);
and

(b) The packages containing such merchandise are inspected and mailed under customs supervision.

A waiver of the right to withdraw the package from the
mails shall be endorsed on each package to be so exported and
signed by the exporter.

An export entry or a warehouse withdrawal for exportation, whichever is appropriate, shall be filed for merchandise
being exported, except for merchandise imported by mail which
is either:

(a) Unclaimed or refused and being returned by the postal
service to the country of origin as undeliverable mail; or

(b) For which a formal entry has not been filed and which
is being remailed from continuous customs or postal custody
to Canada.

Delivery to customs custody for exportation. In the following cases where merchandise has not been in continuous

government custody, delivery to customs custody is appropriate before exportation by mail:

(a) Articles exported for repairs or alterations;

(b) Articles exported for processing;

(c) Merchandise that was imported free of duty under a personal exemption, found to be unsatisfactory, and is being exported for replacement;

(d) Exportation of imported merchandise that was entered under a temporary bond; or

(e) Exportation of defective imported merchandise, with drawback of duties.

Chapter 8

CLEARANCE OF GOODS

Shipments by Air or Sea and from Contiguous Countries

Merchandise is imported when the vessel laden with the goods arrives within a customs port with intent to discharge the cargo. If the merchandise arrives within the limits of the United States by means other than by vessel, then the time of arrival of the conveyance within its borders determines the date of importation.

All arrangements for customs clearance can be made by an importer or someone he designates to act for him. Either the importer or an agent or broker must present the necessary documents to the United States Customs Service to make an entry. It is usually accomplished by an original bill of lading or certificate of the carrier, a commercial invoice, and a special customs invoice for dutiable merchandise.

Usually, the customhouse broker makes an entry at the customhouse after the goods reach the United States for a single entry bond for one shipment or a term bond for several shipments.

An entry can be made by a consignee, his agents, or his authorized regular employees. The only persons who are authorized by the tariff laws of the United States to act as agents for importers are customhouse brokers who will prepare and file the necessary customs documents, arrange for the payment of duties due, effect the release of the merchandise from customs custody, and represent the importer with customs matters.

Each entry must be supported by evidence of the right to make entry; further, a customs power of attorney is usually requested by the customs broker for the person or firm for whom he is representing or acting as agent (Customs Form 5291).

If the entry is made in the name of the broker as importer of record and if the import specialist finds that there is an advanced value or rate advance of the shipment, the broker will be responsible for the payment of additional duties to the U.S. Customs Service.

However, a broker will be relieved of payment of duty if he obtains an owner's declaration, in which case the owner agrees to pay the increased additional duty.

Entry of goods may be made by a nonresident individual or partnership, or a foreign corporation through an agent or representative of the exporter in the United States, or a member of the partnership, or any officer of the corporation.

The surety on any customs bond required from such a nonresident individual or organization must be incorporated in the United States. In addition, a foreign corporation in whose name merchandise is entered must have a resident agent authorized to accept service of process in its behalf in the state where the port of entry is located.

Special Permits for Immediate Delivery Prior to Entry

Applications for special permits for the delivery of imported articles prior to entry shall be made in duplicate on Customs Form 3461, to the satisfaction of the district director of customs. If so, a special permit may be granted to cover the delivery prior to the entry of the merchandise for such permit and importation during a period not to exceed one year. A single entry bond has to be filed on Customs Form 7551, or a term bond on Customs Form 7553 with approved corporate surety. For a single entry for immediate delivery and consumption entry, a bond is required equal to the entered value plus the estimated duties and taxes.

Where there are multiple entries on an immediate and consumption entry bond (term), the amount of $10,000, or a larger amount, may be demanded by the district director at the time of entry.

An immediate delivery entry should be made within ten working days after the day on which the articles are released. If the entry is not made within the prescribed time and the merchandise is unloaded from a carrier it must be ordered into general order storage (bonded warehouse or public stores) at the expense of the consignee until entry is made and proper documents are produced, or a bond given for its production.

If the importer is delinquent in the payment of his customs bills this privilege may be suspended for a specific time or until the bills are paid. If the importer pays all the customs bills for which he is delinquent within five working days after the date of notice of suspension, it may be lifted and privileges reinstated.

Warehouse Entries

Should the importer decide to place his shipment in a bonded warehouse under a warehouse entry, the merchandise can remain in the warehouse up to a period of three years from the date of importation. During the three-year period the merchandise may be reexported without the payment of duty or may be withdrawn for consumption upon the payment of duty at the rate in effect at the time of withdrawal. The owner of the merchandise is required to post a bond in an amount equal to double the estimated amount of duties and taxes.

While in a bonded warehouse the merchandise may be manipulated under customs supervision by cleaning, sorting, and repacking. However, the manipulation must not amount to a manufacture of the merchandise. After manipulation the goods may be exported within the warehousing period without the payment of duty, or one can exercise the alternative to withdraw the merchandise for consumption upon the payment of duty at the time the merchandise is withdrawn.

The merchandise may be transported in bond to another port of entry and entered there under the same conditions as at a port of arrival. Arrangements for transporting goods to an interior port may be made by the consignee, carrier or customhouse broker.

Appraisement Entries

These are informal entries not exceeding $250 in value. An application for such entry may be approved by the port or district director of customs. This is usually requested where the value of the articles cannot be declared, e.g., articles that are second hand, articles that have become deteriorated or damaged before importation (damaged on the voyage of importation, by fire or marine casualty, or any other cause without fault on the part of the shipper), except articles that are not subject of a commercial transaction. It also would apply to household effects used abroad and not intended for sale, personal effects, articles sent by persons in foreign countries as gifts to persons in the United States, tools of

43

trade of a person arriving in the United States, and personal effects of citizens of the United States who have died in a foreign country.

Consumption Entries

These are usually made for the expressed purpose of obtaining delivery of the merchandise for sale or distribution as soon as there has been an examination and release thereof by the customs authorities. The necessary documents must be presented at the customhouse in order to make an entry. If the merchandise is free of duty no special customs invoice is necessary. However, a commercial invoice and an original bill of lading or carrier's certificate must be presented.

Other Types of Entries

I. T. (Immediate Transportation). Merchandise arriving at one point is released on condition that it be transported in bond to another port.

T. E. (Transportation and Exportation). Merchandise passing through the United States on the way to Canada that will be released on condition that it be transported in bond out of the United States.

T. I. B. (Temporary Importation Bond).

P. E. (Permanent Exhibition).

It is required that the consignee or owner shall, in all cases, furnish any bills or statements of cost relating to the article, or that he has no other information in order to make a formal entry thereof.

Invoicing

1. A special customs invoice must be prepared for each shipment to the United States of goods that are dutiable for over $500. (Customs Form 5515.) Special customs invoices are divided into two classes: They apply to those goods acquired by purchase or agreement to purchase, or cover goods other than purchase or agreement to purchase (consignment).

Special customs invoices should state the following: Each item of the merchandise should be correctly described on the special customs invoice, stating the unit price currently paid or agreed to be paid. The invoice must state the charges and fees that are included in the unit price and those charges and fees that are not included. The invoice should state the weights and measures of the country or the place from which the merchandise is shipped, or in the weights and measures of the United States as per pound, yard, dozen or gross. Any rebate, drawback allowed on exportation and any bounty or grant bestowed upon the manufacture, production or exportation of the goods must be itemized on the invoice by name and amount. The invoice must state whether the production of the goods involved as to costs for "assists" were incurred by the importer of the merchandise or some other person, e.g., dies, molds, tooling, printing, plates, engineering work, financial assistance of any kind. If assists were made the value should be stated by whom supplied. If supplied without costs, to be invoiced separately. All charges and fees upon the goods must be specified by name, e.g., buying commission, selling commission, insurance, freight charges and other particulars affecting the dutiable and nondutiable charges.

2. A commercial invoice prepared in the same manner customary for a commercial transaction is acceptable for customs purposes for goods exempted from the requirements of a special customs invoice. Commercial invoices are usually sent to the importer by the seller or shipper of the merchandise, indicating the name and address of the supplier abroad and the necessary particulars, i.e., description of the merchandise, unit price, extension, and all other terms that are essential for proper classification and appraisement.

3. If the required special customs or commercial invoice is not filed at the time the goods are entered, a pro forma invoice must be filed at the time of entry and a bond given for the production of the required invoice not later than six months from the date of entry, or the forfeiture of the bond (liquidated damage). When a commercial invoice is not available at the time of entry, the broker will give a bond for the missing document as herein stated. He will submit a pro forma invoice issued by the importer that will describe the impending shipment as to all necessary particulars, which is tantamount to a complete commercial invoice.

It is advisable to prepare invoices in the English language. However, an invoice prepared in the language of the country of exportation should have an accurate English translation.

Goods assembled for shipment to the same consignee by

one vessel or conveyance may be included in one invoice. Installments of a shipment covered by a single order and shipped by one supplier to one consignee may be included in one invoice if the installments arrive at the port of entry by any means of transportation within a period not to exceed seven consecutive days.

Designation and Examination of Merchandise

The port or district director of customs usually designates for examination one carton of every shipment, or less than 10 or 10 percent of the shipment. However, where the contents of a large shipment consists of several kinds of merchandise, the district or port director, when deemed expedient, may order certain samples from the shipment in lieu of the usual designation. Samples are usually requested for bulk shipments.

In order to examine the merchandise, the import specialist has to determine the following factors: (a) Value of goods, (b) dutiable status, (c) marking country of origin, (d) if prohibited article, (e) whether goods have been truly and correctly invoiced, (f) whether goods are in excess or shortage of the invoice quantities, (g) whether some of the goods imported meet the requirements of law as to fitness for human consumption, (h) certain kinds of goods will be weighed, gauged, or measured.

Inflammable, explosive, or other dangerous merchandise or any merchandise that cannot conveniently be examined at the public stores shall be examined at the place of arrival, pier, wharf, or importer's premises, or other suitable place; all other merchandise shall be examined at the public stores unless approved by the district or port director to be examined elsewhere.

If the examination is requested other than at the public stores, the importer is required to execute a bond (Customs Form 7551 or 7553) containing a condition for the return of the merchandise after its release from customs custody upon the completion of the final examination for the purpose of appraisement.

If the invoice or entry does not state these facts, the expense of ascertaining them may be collected from the consignee before release from customs custody.

If there is a failure to enter the goods either at the port

of arrival or at an interior port within five working days after the arrival, the district or port director will place them in a general order warehouse at the risk and expense of the importer. (A general order warehouse is a bonded warehouse where the merchandise is stored.)

If the goods are not entered within one year from the date of importation, the merchandise becomes subject to sale at a public auction and the importer of record must be notified. However, if the charges and duty, if any, are paid before the date of the auction, the merchandise may be released if it is not prohibited or restricted.

Perishable goods, or goods liable to depreciation, and explosive substances that remain not entered may be sold.

Accumulation of Charges

Storage charges, expenses of sale, Internal Revenue taxes imposed upon or by reason of importation, duties, and amounts for the satisfaction of liens must be taken out of the money obtained on the sale of unentered goods. Any surplus remaining after these deductions is ordinarily payable to the holder of a duly endorsed bill of lading covering the goods. If the goods are subject to Internal Revenue taxes imposed upon or by reason of importation, and if they will not bring enough monies on sale at a public auction to pay such Internal Revenue taxes, they are subject to destruction.

Analysis of Samples

The import specialist submits to the chief chemist of the laboratory samples of all articles requiring technical analysis, such as textiles, chemicals, minerals, and others, for a report as to any facts necessary to the proper appraisement and advisory classification of such articles.

Appraising officers shall retain samples of the merchandise when advisory classification is at a rate of duty higher than the entered value or when, for any reason, it is probable that a protest of the classification of the merchandise will be filed.

Chapter 9

ELEMENTS THAT AFFECT DUTIABLE VALUE

It is in the best interest of both the shipper and the im porter of merchandise to be aware of the charges that ai dutiable and nondutiable and how they will affect the dutiab value of the merchandise. The elements included in this chaj ter provides a simple explanation of the manner in which tl duties are applied.

"Dutiable charges" are such costs and other expens as are incidental to placing the merchandise in conditic packed ready for shipment to the United States. Such charg must represent the actual cost and be confined solely to me chandise exported to the United States. Any expenses tl enter into the value of the merchandise when sold in the orc nary course of trade for domestic consumption in the count of exportation are not charges but become part of the value the merchandise. The cost of material and labor in connecti with the packing of the goods for shipment is part of the dutial value.

"Nondutiable charges" are such items of cost and exper as constitute no part of the value of the merchandise when s in the ordinary course of trade in the country of exportati and are no part of the expense of placing it in condition, pacl ready for shipment to the United States (cost, insurance, ; freight). Ocean freight, port fees, and marine insurance ; usually considered nondutiable charges and do not form p of value. Inland freight from the factory to the pier is a n dutiable item.

"Ex-factory Sales" are those where the seller pla the goods at the disposal of the buyer at the factory, at agreed price and time, and all charges and risks of the go from the time that they are so placed at his disposal are the buyer's account and are not dutiable when exported to United States. However, inland freight from the factory abr to the principal market is a dutiable item and is an integ part of the value.

Packing

In order to expedite matters, importers should advise their shippers or suppliers to indicate on their commercial invoice or packing list the quantity of each item of goods in each case, package, box or bale, and place marks and numbers on each so that they are identified on the invoice or packing list opposite each item. If they cooperate in this respect, it will be easy for customs to decide which container should be opened for examination, and it will also facilitate verification of the contents of the entire shipment. Further, it will minimize the possibility that the importer may be asked to redeliver for further examination a package that has been released to him.

The import specialist cannot appraise the cost of containers or coverings. He is required to ascertain or estimate the "costs" of containers and other costs, charges and expenses relative thereto. The actual cost of the containers should be included in the final appraised value, even though the addition of such costs may increase the value of the contents sufficiently to subject them to a higher rate of duty. This is realized after ascertaining the dutiable value of the merchandise, which would be the wholesale price of the goods, plus the cost of packing, and that cost should be added to the wholesale price.

Drums

Drums for imported merchandise (coal tar products) if imported empty are treated as imported articles and subject to duty unless specifically exempt. If not imported empty, not designed for, or capable of reuse, they are subject to the same rate as their contents if of foreign origin. However, the cost of drums are free of duty if proved to be United States goods returned without having been advanced in value or improved in condition by any means while abroad.

The usual or ordinary types of drums or holders if designed for, or capable of, reuse are subject to treatment as imported articles separate and distinct from their contents. Such holders or containers are not part of the dutiable value of their contents and are separately subject to duty upon each and every importation unless specifically exempt from duty.

International Traffic

Lift vans, cargo vans, shipping tanks, skids, pallets, and similar instruments, arriving loaded or empty, in use or to be used in the shipment of merchandise in international traffic, have been designated by the commissioner of customs as "instruments of international traffic." Such instruments may be released generally without entry or the payment of duty.

These modern means of transportation have been an impetus in the movement of goods from manufacturer to consignee, whether by land, air, or water and without regard to distance. This led to the evolution of "containerization." This method reduces costs of transporting merchandise as well as damage and pilferage. The district director of customs may assign a container station or the importer's premises for examination. Entry permits have to be obtained and they require a special "containerized cargo bond."

Commingling of Merchandise

Whenever articles subject to different rates of duty are packed together so that the quantity or value of each class of merchandise cannot be readily ascertained by customs (without physical segregation of the shipment or the contents of any package thereof) the commingled articles shall be subject to the highest rate of duty applicable to any part of the commingled lot unless the consignee or his agent segregates the merchandise under customs supervision.

Due consideration will be given where there is a commingled lot and part is commercially negligible, or is not capable of being segregated without excessive cost, and will not be segregated prior to its use in a manufacturing process or otherwise, and that the commingling was not intended to avoid the payment of duty. This is realized if the consignee or agent furnishes satisfactory proof prescribed by the secretary of the treasury.

Excess

If any package that has been designated for examination is found by the customs officer to contain any article not specified in the invoice, and there is reason to believe that such article was omitted from the invoice with fraudulent intent on the part of the seller, the contents of the entire package in which the excess goods are found may be subject to seizure and possible forfeiture.

Where no fraud is apparent, fines and penalties do not accrue. However, the duties on the excess goods will be collected.

Shortage

When a deficiency in weight or measure is found by the customs officer in the examination of any package that has been designated for examination, an allowance in duty will be made for the deficiency.

A claim against the government may be allowed if the importer or the bonded carrier executes Customs Form 5931 and attaches copies of the dock receipts or other documents evidencing the nonreceipt of the lost or missing package and files it with customs. The claim must be filed within ninety days from the date of liquidation, or within one year from the date of entry, whichever is longer. Any claim received after that time will not be acknowledged.

If the importing carrier refuses to sign the form, the importer may nevertheless file the form without the carrier's signature, but he should indicate in the form the name of the individual employee of the importing carrier who refused to sign. If unable to obtain this, the importer should attach a statement to that effect.

Damage or Deterioration

An article has been held to be "damaged" when its value, its usefulness, or its efficiency is only impaired, and an article is considered "destroyed" when its value or usefulness is completely lost.

Merchandise in a shipment arriving in the United States found to be damaged or deteriorated and entirely without commercial value is treated as a "nonimportation" and is not assessable for duty. If part of the shipment is damaged or deteriorated, an allowance for duty will be permitted if the importer segregates the affected parts from the remainder of the shipment under customs supervision.

When a shipment consists of perishable merchandise,

an allowance cannot be made unless within ninety-six hours after the unloading of the merchandise and before it has been removed from customs custody, the importer files an application for an allowance with the district or port director. As for shipments of iron or steel, an allowance will not be made for partial damage because of discoloration or rust.

Drawbacks

Drawback exists when a duty or tax that has been collected is refunded in whole or in part because of the particular use made of the commodity on which the duty or tax was collected.

One should apply for a drawback under Sec. 1313(a) of U.S. Code Annotated Title 19, by filing an application with the regional commissioner of customs for a rate of drawback. Customs Form 4477 should be used for this purpose. The word "rate" means authorization to claim and receive drawback.

The claimant of a drawback should establish that the articles were in fact exported. Claims must be filed within three years after exportation of the article.

The exportation of imported merchandise after it has been released from customs custody does not result in a refund of the duties paid on the merchandise. There are three exceptions to a refund of duties paid at the time of entry for the exportation of imported merchandise after it has been released from customs custody.

1. When articles manufactured or produced in the United States with the use of imported merchandise are exported, a refund of 99 percent of the duties paid on the imported merchandise is refundable as drawback.

2. When imported goods do not conform to the sample or specifications as ordered, or were shipped without the consent of the consignee, he may secure a refund of 99 percent of the duties paid by returning the goods to customs custody within ninety days (or longer if authorized) after they were released and exported under customs supervision.

3. When imported merchandise found not to be entitled to admission into commerce of the United States is exported or destroyed under customs supervision, a refund of the entire amount of duties paid on the rejected merchandise is allowable.

A refund of the entire amount of duties is allowed when

imported goods are exported from a bonded customs warehouse, or from continuous customs custody, or when the imported goods found not to be entitled to admission into the commerce of the United States are destroyed under customs supervision.

A refund of the entire amount of duties may also be made when the articles under bond, under any provision of the customs law, are destroyed under customs supervision during the period of the bond and when articles in a customs bonded warehouse are voluntarily abandoned to the government by the consignee.

Countervailing Duty

This applies when a foreign country bestows a bounty or grant on any article of merchandise exported to the United States, regardless of whether or not the payment or bestowal is made upon the manufacturer on the production of the merchandise and regardless of whether it is made directly or indirectly.

The secretary of the treasury ascertains and determines what shall be the net amount of each bounty or grant. The countervailing duty order is issued by the commissioner of customs.

The law states that the amount to be paid shall have an additional duty equal to the net amount of bounty or grant.

Under the old law there was no time limit within which the secretary of the treasury had to make its determination. The trade act of 1974 directs him to initiate a formal investigation to determine whether or not a bounty or grant is being paid upon the filing of a notice. Within six months he must make a preliminary determination and then six months from that date, a final determination.

Foreign-Trade Zone in the United States

Such zones offer many advantages to foreign exporters and importers who can lawfully bring in merchandise that may be stored, assembled, distributed, repacked, sold mixed with foreign and domestic merchandise, manipulated, or manufactured. For example: an article that is embroidered is brought into the foreign-trade zone; the embroidery could be removed and a lesser amount of duty would be paid after the merchandise is entered at the customhouse. The foreign exporter can use the alternative of either exporting the goods or transferring it into customs. The merchandise can be held for an unlimited period without payment of duty waiting for a favorable market.

If entered for consumption at the customhouse, the merchandise will be assessed for duty and taxes as other foreign imported merchandise.

Another outstanding advantage is that the merchandise may be exhibited within the foreign-trade zone without bond and with no requirement of exportation or duty payment. Further, he is not limited to a mere display of samples, but he may sell from stock in wholesale quantities. Savings in shipping charges can be realized in that unassembled items can be reassembled in the zone.

Merchandise may be removed or relabeled in the zone to conform to requirements of entry standards. However, remarking or relabeling that would be misleading is not permitted in the zone.

Where imported merchandise has been kept in a customs bonded warehouse, it has a certain limited time on its retention. However, before expiration date, a transfer to the zone may be made only for the purpose of eventual exportation or destruction. When the transfer takes place, the bond is cancelled and all obligations in regard to duty payment or as to the time when the merchandise is to be reexported are terminated.

For the Atlantic coast, the old Brooklyn Navy Yard (formerly located on Staten Island) is the only foreign trade zone available. Others are located at the ports of Bay City, Michigan; Honolulu, Hawaii; New Orleans, Louisiana; San Francisco, California; Sault Sainte Marie, Michigan; Seattle, Washington; Toledo, Ohio; and Mayaguez, Puerto Rico.

Insular Possessions

Guam, Wake Island, Midway Islands, Kingman Reef, Johnston Island, and American Samoa are American territory, but not within the customs territory of the United States. Importations into these islands are not governed by the Tariff Act of 1930 or the customs regulations.

When articles are coming directly into the United States from an insular possession other than Puerto Rico, in a shipment valued over twenty-five dollars and subject to be admitted

54

free of duty, relating to articles produced in such insular possessions, there then shall be filed a certificate of origin to show that the merchandise is the growth and product of such possession or of the United States or both and does not contain foreign materials to the value of more than 50 percent of its total value. Such certificate shall not be required for any shipment valued at twenty-five dollars or less. Public Law 94-88 of August 9, 1975, states that the foreign-value material limitation has been increased from 50 percent to 70 percent, which is allowed on watches and watch movements.

All laws affecting imports of articles, goods, wares and merchandise from foreign countries shall apply to articles, goods, wares and merchandise, and persons coming from the Canal Zone, Isthmus of Panama.

In determining whether an article produced or manufactured in any such insular possession contains foreign materials to the value of more than 50 percent, a comparison shall be made between the actual purchase price of the foreign materials (excluding any material that at the time such article is entered, or withdrawn from warehouse for consumption in the United States, may be imported into the United States from a foreign country, other than Cuba, or the Philippine Republic free of duty) plus the cost of transportation to such insular possession and any charges that may accrue after landing, and the final appraised value in the United States determined in accordance with Sec. 402 of the Tariff Act of 1930, as amended, of the article brought into the United States.

Agents

Agents play a very important part in the consummation of transactions on behalf of their principals in foreign countries. Where an agent represents an importer, the commission is deemed to be a buying commission, and it is not included in the dutiable value. Whereas, if the agent represents the manufacturer or seller generally, it is deemed to be a selling commission and is included as part of the dutiable value.

There are some agents who buy merchandise for their own account and sell at an intermediate profit. Technically they are considered principals and the monies realized for such service are also part of the dutiable value.

Currency

When it is necessary for customs officers, for the purpose of comparing prices or values, to convert foreign currency to United States dollars, such conversion shall be made at the rate of exchange in effect on the date of exportation of the merchandise under appraisement. For example: if merchandise is invoiced in a foreign currency but payable in United States dollars at the rate of one dollar for eight units of the foreign currency, the transaction is in United States currency. If the converse applies, the appraisement would be in a foreign currency.

The rate or rates of exchange to be used for customs purposes for any day of exportation within the quarter shall be the rate or rates as certified and published, unless the rate or rates certified by the Federal Reserve Bank for the day of exportation vary by 5 percent or more from such first certified and published rate or rates.

Taxes

Where the home consumption tax applies only to the sales of goods made for home consumption, the tax is not applicable to goods made only for export. (Sec. 402a.)

A tax that is applied on the exportation of the merchandise but does not apply on such merchandise when remaining or sold in the country of exportation, does not constitute a part of export value. (Sec. 402a.)

Where a tax is paid by the consuming purchaser, such tax is not included in the appraised foreign value. (Sec. 402a.)

C.I.F. Price

Where merchandise is freely offered and sold for export at a price C.I.F. (cost, insurance, and freight) New York, duty paid under Sec. 402a, the export value as defined by law would be the net value after the nondutiable charges and duty are deducted. The definitions of value do not contemplate a freely offered C.I.F. duty-paid price without allowing deductions of nondutiable charges to be the net value for duty purposes.

F.O.B. Sale

An F.O.B. sale (free on board export carrier at the port of export) is one in which the seller's unit price includes all costs and risks of the goods until such time as they are delivered on board the exporting carrier.

Time of Exportation

The time of exportation referred to in Sec. 402 and Sec. 402a of the Tariff Act of 1930, as amended, is the date on which the merchandise actually leaves the country of exportation for the United States. However, if the merchandise is not exported directly by water and there is no positive evidence at hand as to the date of exportation, the date of the special customs or commercial invoice shall be considered to be the date of exportation unless the invoice appears to be dated after the date the merchandise actually left the country of exportation.

Chapter 10

IMPORT QUOTAS

Definitions

    <u>Absolute Quotas</u> are those which permit a limited number of units of specified merchandise to be entered or withdrawn for consumption during specified periods. Once the quantity permitted under the quota is filled, no further entries or withdrawals for consumption of merchandise subject to quota are permitted. Some absolute quotas limit the entry or withdrawal of merchandise from particular countries (geographic quotas) while others are global quotas and limit the entry or withdrawal of merchandise not by source but by total quantity.

    <u>Tariff-Rate Quotas</u> permit a specified quantity of merchandise to be entered or withdrawn for consumption at a reduced duty rate during a specified period.

Enactment and Administration of Quotas

    (a) Tariff-rate quotas and absolute quotas are established by presidential proclamation, executive orders, and legislative enactment.

    (b) The administration of quotas vary by the type of commodity involved, the country of exportation, the period or periods the quota is opened, and the type of quota. Quotas are divided into two categories: quotas administered directly by the U.S. Customs Service, and quotas administered by other agencies which are enforced by the U.S. Customs Service, and which may require special procedures or special documentation in accordance with the regulation and direction of the particular agency involved.

    (c) At the opening of the quota no importer shall be permitted to present entries or withdrawals for consumption of quota-class merchandise for a quantity in excess of the quantity admissible under the applicable quota.

Merchandise Imported in Excess of Quota Quantities

(a) Absolute quota merchandise imported in excess of the quantity admissible under the applicable quotas may be disposed of in accordance with paragraph (c) of this section.

(b) Tariff-rate quota merchandise imported in excess of the quantity admissible at the reduced quota rate under a tariff-rate quota is permitted entry at the higher duty rate. However, it may be disposed of in accordance with paragraph (c) of this section.

(c) Disposition of excess merchandise imported in excess of either an absolute or a tariff-rate quota may be held for the opening of the next quota period by placing it in a foreign-trade zone or by entering it for warehouse, or it may be exported or destroyed under customs supervision.

Filled Quotas for Mail Entries

Any package containing merchandise subject to an absolute quota that is filled shall be returned to the postmaster for immediate return to the sender as undeliverable mail. The addressee will be notified that entry has been denied because the quota is filled.

Unless a formal entry or entry by appraisement is required, a mail entry shall be issued and forwarded with the package to the postmaster for delivery to the addressee and collection of any duties in the same manner as for any mail package subject to customs treatment.

Commodities Subject to Import Quotas

Coffee. The United States is a signatory to the International Coffee Agreement. Under the provisions of the agreement, coffee from nonmember countries is subject to an import quota. The U.S. Customs Service administers this absolute quota.

Textile articles. The U.S. Customs Service administers import controls on certain cotton, wool, and manmade fiber articles manufactured or produced in designated countries. The controls are imposed on the basis of directives issued to the commissioner of customs by the chairman of the Committee for the Implementation of Textile Agreements.

Information concerning specific import controls in effect

may be obtained from the commissioner of customs. Other information concerning the textile program may be obtained from the Chairman, Committee for the Implementation of Textile Agreements, U.S. Department of Commerce, Washington, D.C. 20230.

Candy. Sugar regulations, issued by the Department of Agriculture under authority contained in the Sugar Act of 1948, as amended, establish a quota on sweetened chocolate, candy, and confectionery. The customs service administers the candy and confectionery quota.

Quotas Administered by Other Government Agencies

Fuel oil and certain oil products. The Department of the Interior administers import quotas on fuel oil and certain oil products on a licensing basis. Information concerning the licensing requirements on such products may be obtained from the Director, Office of Oil and Gas, U.S. Department of the Interior, Washington, D.C. 20240.

Watches, and watch movements from insular possessions. The Departments of Interior and Commerce administer the import quotas on watches and watch movements from insular possessions admissible free of duty on a licensing basis. Information concerning licenses may be obtained from the Office of Import Programs, Special Import Programs Division, U.S. Department of Commerce, Washington, D.C. 20230.

Sugar. The secretary of agriculture (under the Sugar Act of 1948, as amended) establishes quotas on sugar and sugar-containing products or mixtures from foreign countries and for sugar brought in from the Virgin Islands, Hawaii, and Puerto Rico.

Detailed information regarding the procedure for entering quota sugar or for entering quota-exempt sugar for reexport for livestock feed, etc., may be obtained from the Quota and Allotment Branch, Sugar Division, Agricultural Stabilization and Conservation Service, U.S. Department of Agricultutre, Washington, D.C. 20250.

Dairy products. Certain dairy products are subject to annual import quotas administered by the Department of Agriculture and may be imported only under import licenses issued by that department. Detailed information on the licensing of these products, or the conditions under which limited quantities may be imported without licenses, may be obtained from the Import Branch, Foreign Agricultural Service, U.S. Department of Agriculture, Washington, D.C. 20250.

Chapter 11

FACTORS TO BE CONSIDERED BY IMPORTER

In order to cope with the U.S. Customs Service, shippers and importers must bear in mind that it is incumbent upon them to fully cooperate in furnishing all pertinent information on their invoices relative to their transactions in order to determine the proper appraisal of the merchandise in the entry of their goods. The highlights are the purchase price in the country of purchase, relationship of the parties, buyer and seller, commissions or fees paid to the agent, discounts, taxes, materials, designs, molds or other assists given to the supplier or manufacturer by the importer.

When the import specialist requests a sample of merchandise of an imported entry on Customs Form 28 that had not been ordered for examination by the district director, and the importer fails to submit it, and if it is found to be advanced in the rate of duty, the importer is precluded from invoking a protest within Section 520 (c) (1) of the Tariff Act of 1930, as amended.

The importer is also precluded from seeking relief where he or his customs broker was delinquent in responding to a written request by the import specialist for information as to the value of certain goods in a shipment on the grounds that the appraisement was the result of a mistake of fact, clerical error, or inadvertence and offers proof that a lower value is warranted. The reasoning applied is that if the appraisement is erroneous it was caused by the deliberate failure of the importer or the broker to furnish the necessary information.

Should a foreign shipper manufacture goods with foreign material, and some additional material is supplied by the importer for the production of the articles, and the shipper invoices the articles and states only the actual cost of the materials to the manufacturer without including the value of the materials supplied by the importer, the material submitted by the importer in the production of the articles is known as an "assist." It is considered a part of the cost of production of the completed article, which should be added to the cost of manufacturing the article.

Failure to make such a statement as to the "assist" may lead to a fraud case within Sec. 592 of the Tariff Act of 1930, as amended, or Sec. 1592 of the U.S. Code, subject to fines and penalties.

Foreign shippers should not assume that certain charges, such as commissions, are nondutiable; they should be stated on the invoice proper. They may be selling commissions, which are dutiable, compared to buying commissions, which are generally nondutiable.

In the case of a foreign shipper who purchases goods from a manufacturer abroad and then sells them to an importer, at a delivered price, and who fails to show the costs of the goods to him on the invoice, the transaction between the shipper and manufacturer may be one of a selling commission, or else it might be an intermediate profit for the shipper. All particulars should be stated on the invoice to permit the customs authorities to ascertain the proper dutiable value of the merchandise.

Should a foreign manufacturer ship replacement goods to an importer in the United States and invoice the goods at the net price without showing the full price less the allowance for the defective goods previously shipped and returned, the failure to do so may lead to further inquiries by the import specialist from the importer to determine the proper valuation of the merchandise.

Where a foreign shipper indicates on the invoice that the importer is the purchaser, whereas, he is in fact either an agent who is receiving a commission for selling the goods or a party who will receive part of the proceeds of the sale of the goods sold for the joint account of the shipper and consignee, the omission to state all the particulars may lead to a fraud case since there are alleged misrepresentations or concealments of material matters.

Should a foreign shipper sell goods at a list price, less a discount, and invoice them at the net price and fail to show the discount, this is misleading to the import specialist for he has to determine all terms of the sale. Where these facts exist the import specialist will check his records and will delay the final completion of the appraised value of the shipment.

Further, not all discounts are allowed by customs; cash discounts are allowed, including those discounts that are freely offered to all purchasers.

Should a foreign shipper state on an invoice of purchased goods that the current market value in the foreign country is the same as the purchase price, whereas, there have been sales for home consumption or export at a higher price between the date of purchase and the date of exportation, the appraised value of the goods would be governed at the time of exportation to the United States.

It is incumbent on the importer or his authorized agent to make a signed declaration on the entry that all statements that appear thereon, and all other documents that are part of the entry, are true and correct in every respect including values and quantities and that no other invoice or document shows a different price, value, or quantity and to his knowledge none exists.

When an importer believes that a clerical error, mistake of fact, or other inadvertence has taken place in an entry, appraisement, liquidation, or other transaction and that he is being assessed more duties than are correct, he can ask for administrative review of the action. He must file his request within specified time limits, as follows.

If an error described in the above provision is made by the importer, he is limited to the period within one year commencing from the date in which the transaction reflecting that error first occurred, or ninety days after the date of a liquidation or exaction reflecting that error if the liquidation or exaction is made more than nine months after the date of entry.

If the error is made originally by customs in a liquidation, reliquidation, or exaction, and is not traceable to an error made by the importer in an earlier entry or other transaction, the importer will be entitled to a full year from the date of the liquidation, reliquidation, or exaction to file his petition within Sec. 520 (c) (1) of the Tariff Act of 1930 and will not be subject to the ninety-day limitation applicable in circumstances where the error was made by the importer.

If the import specialist does not agree with the contentions of the importer and is sustained at applicable review levels, the importer is usually notified in writing that his claim has been denied. He then has protest rights against the decision and may have the issued resolved by the customs court.

When an importer anticipates the possibility of litigation in the United States Customs Court, it is always feasible to issue Customs Form 19 in lieu of Sec. 520 (c) (1) within the statutory period in which the import specialist will decide the issue on its merits. An application for further review should be filed on Customs Form 20 and directed to the Commissioner of Customs in Washington, D. C., Director of Classification and Value Div., Dept. of the Treasury, U. S. Customs Service, within the period of ninety days allowed for protest. After liquidation, customs officials will have two years from the date the protest is filed to review the protest and allow or deny it in whole or in part.

When a protest has been denied after Customs Form 20 has been reviewed, if all liquidated duties have been paid, an action may be commenced in the U. S. Customs Court by filing a summons within 180 days after the denial of the protest.

Chapter 12

CLASSIFICATION OF MERCHANDISE

Application of the Tariff Act

The customs officer in examining imported merchandise must determine the provision of the Tariff Act that applies in order to ascertain the proper rate of duty. It is a fundamental principle of customs law that merchandise is classified in the condition that it is imported.

It is well settled that one may process or further manufacture his merchandise before importation (when placed in a foreign-trade zone) so as to take advantage of the most favorable provision of the tariff law.

The full rates of duty apply to the products of the following Communist countries: Albania, Bulgaria, China (Communist-controlled), Czechoslovakia, Estonia, Germany (Soviet zone), Hungary, Indo-China (Communist-controlled), North Korea, Kurile Islands, Latvia, Lithuania, Outer Mongolia, Tibet, and the U.S.S.R. The countries hereinstated do not have the benefits (of the most-favored nations) of reduced rates of the Tariff Act of 1930, as amended.

Classification of merchandise is usually governed by the following principles embraced in the Tariff Act of 1930, as amended:

Congressional intent. The intention of Congress prevails over all other classification rules of construction. Should there be any ambiguity in a statute that has more than one common meaning the legislative history should be resolved in order to determine the congressional intent.

Legislative approval. When a paragraph of a subsequent tariff is enacted in substantially the same language as the language used in the corresponding paragraph of the previous tariff act, such action is commonly known as legislative approval of any judicial interpretation that may have been made of such language.

Designation by use. Determination of chief use shall be made at the time of importation whether or not the tariff provisions explicitly require classification by chief use. Chief use at or immediately prior to time of importation shall be the test regardless of whether the statutory provision is an <u>eo</u> <u>nomine</u> (named) provision implying use or a provision expressly designating chief use for a specific purpose.

Determining chief use in the United States is not confined to such use of imported articles, but to precisely identical or similar merchandise, whether domestic or foreign. For example: Where a trench coat, militarily styled, contained a belt with brass rings that were included in the design of the coat for use and convenience of the wearer in carrying items that were useful such as gloves, keys, and other personal articles, the determination as to classification was that the brass rings were utilitarian rather than ornamental and chief use governed in this case.

<u>Eo nomine designation</u>. The common or commercial meaning of an <u>eo</u> <u>nomine</u> designation must be determined as of the date of the enactment of the latest tariff act. An <u>eo</u> <u>nomine</u> designation is more specific than, and prevails over, a provision for parts of an article, e.g., shirt collars made in part of flax.

<u>Relative specificity</u>. The rule of relative specificity is applied when merchandise is described in two or more competing paragraphs of the tariff act. For example, "Fish packed in oil" is more specific than "fish prepared or preserved not specially provided for," and "napkins in the piece made of linen table damask" is more specific than "table damask."

<u>Commercial common designation</u>. To prove commercial designation, it is essential to show that the statutory phrase or term under consideration had a definite, uniform, and general meaning in the trade and commerce of the United States as of the time of enactment of the tariff act that was different from the ordinary common meaning and then to prove what such commerical meaning was. For example, a fabric must have both warp and weft threads or wires to come within the common meaning of the term "woven."

<u>Component material of chief value</u>. When an article consists of several different components such as paper, plastic, and wood, and there is no provision in the tariff for that article, the component material of chief value will determine the rate of duty applicable to that article.

<u>Entireties</u>. When a "part" of an article is something necessary to the completion of that article, it is a component part, without which the article to which it is to be joined could

not function as such article. For example, furniture composed of wooden frames and wool tapestry coverings (wool tapestry--chief value) is held dutiable as an entirety and classified at the wool tapestry rate. The mere fact that two articles are designed and constructed to be used together does not necessarily make either a part of the other. For example, a camera and tripod, each of which performs its natural function without the aid of the other, is not an entirety.

Change in Classification or Value; Higher or Lower Rate; Effective Date

If there is an established and uniform practice at the various ports, a change in classification resulting in a higher rate of duty, except as the result of a court decision, shall be made upon the bureau's instructions and shall be applicable only to merchandise entered for consumption after the expiration of ninety days after the date of the publication of the bureau's instructions in the "Customs Bulletin and Decisions". In the case of merchandise entered for warehouse, such change shall apply to goods withdrawn for consumption after the expiration of such ninety-day period, provided the warehouse entry is unliquidated or can be reliquidated within ninety days after the date of liquidation.

A change in classification resulting in a lower rate of duty, except as the result of a court decision, shall be made only upon the bureau's instructions or upon the receipt of a Customs Information Exchange report showing the higher classification to be clearly erroneous and contrary to the current practice at the various ports. A change to a lower rate, when decided upon, shall be applicable to all unliquidated entries and to all protested entries involving the same issue that have not been denied in whole or in part. (Customs Information Exchange is a central agency of the U.S. Customs Service for the dissemination of values and classifications to the ports of the United States.)

Should an importer desire to obtain the rate of duty of any article imported, he may write to the district director of customs for information. The importer must furnish him with particulars so that the merchandise can be readily identified for tariff purposes, such as a complete description of the goods with a sample, if possible, and illustrative material such as a catalog when one cannot fully describe the article, method of manufacture, cost of component material of chief value, also chief use in the United States.

67

If the district director is certain that the same or similar article has been classified under an established and uniform practice he will so advise the importer as to the prevailing rate of duty. However, if no established or uniform practice exists, the district director will give an advisory opinion and refer the importer to the commissioner of customs in Washington where the importer will obtain a binding ruling.

Chapter 13

SPECIAL CLASSIFICATION PROVISIONS

Articles Exported and Returned

Products of the United States that are returned after having been exported, without having been advanced in value or improved in condition by any process of manufacture or other means while abroad, are free of duty (Customs Form 3311).

Merchandise upon which duty has been paid and that has been exported and then reimported is liable for duty on every subsequent shipment except the following: Articles previously imported with respect to which the duty was paid upon such previous importation are free of duty if (1) reimported, without having been advanced in value or improved in condition by any process of manufacture or other means while abroad, after having been exported under lease to a foreign manufacturer, and (2) reimported by or for the account of the person who imported it into, and exported it from, the United States.

Articles previously imported with respect to which the duty was paid upon such previous importation are free of duty if (1) exported within three years after the date of such previous importation, (2) reimported without having been advanced in value or improved in condition by any process of manufacture or other means while abroad, (3) reimported for the reason that such articles do not conform to sample or specifications, and (4) reimported by or for the account of the person who imported them into, and exported them from the United States.

Articles returned after having been exported for use temporarily abroad solely for any of the following purposes, if imported by or for the person who exported them, are free of duty:

Exhibition, examination, or experimentation, for scientific or educational purposes;

Exhibition in connection with any circus or menagerie;

Exhibition or use at any public exposition, fair or conference;

In the case of horses, used for racing.

Samples for Soliciting Orders: Articles Admitted Free of Duty under Bond

Item #860.30 of the Tariff Act of 1930, as amended, provides that any sample (except alcoholic beverages and tobacco products) valued not over one dollar each, or marked, torn, perforated, or otherwise treated so that it is unsuitable for sale or for use otherwise than as a sample, to be used in the United States only for soliciting orders for products of foreign countries, is free of duty.

Alcoholic beverages. Each sample (containing not more than eight ounces if of malt beverage, no more than four ounces if a wine, and not more than two ounces if any other alcoholic beverage) to be used in the United States by persons importing alcoholic beverages in commercial quantities is free of duty and exempt from the internal revenue tax.

Tobacco products, cigarette papers and tubes. Each sample (consisting of not more than three cigars, three cigarettes, one-eighth ounce of tobacco, one-eighth ounce of snuff, three cigarette tubes, or twenty-five cigarette papers) to be used in the United States only for soliciting orders by persons importing tobacco products, cigarette papers, or cigarette tubes in commercial quantities is free of duty and exempt from the internal revenue tax.

Samples: Articles Admitted Free of Duty under Bond

Certain goods when not imported for sale or approval may be admitted into the United States without the payment of duty under bond for their exportation within one year from the date of importation, not to exceed three years at the discretion of the secretary of the treasury.

All samples of the merchandise included in the following items are free of duty under bond:

Models of women's wearing apparel imported by manufacturers for use solely as models in their own establishments;

Articles imported by illustrators and photographers for use solely as models in their own establishments, in the illustrating of catalogs, pamphlets, or advertising matter;

Samples solely for use in taking orders for merchandise;

70

Articles solely for examination with a view to reproduction, or for such examination and reproduction (except photoengraved printing plates for examination and reproduction); and motion-picture advertising films;

Articles intended solely for testing, experimental, or review purposes, including plans, specifications, drawings, blueprints, photographs, and similar articles for use in connection with experiments or for study;

Automobiles, motorcycles, bicycles, airships, balloons, boats, racing shells, and similar vehicles and craft, and the usual equipment of the foregoing; all the foregoing that are brought temporarily into the United States by nonresidents for the purpose of taking part in races or other specific contests;

Locomotives and other railroad equipment brought temporarily into the United States for use in clearing obstructions, fighting fires, or making emergency repairs on railroads within the United States, or for use in transportation otherwise than in international traffic when the secretary of the treasury finds that the temporary use of foreign railroad equipment is necessary to meet an emergency;

Containers for compressed gases, filled or empty, and containers or other articles in use for covering or holding merchandise (including personal or household effects) during transportation and suitable for reuse for that purpose;

Articles of special design for temporary use exclusively in connection with the manufacture or production of articles for export;

Animals and poultry brought into the United States for the purpose of breeding, exhibition, or competition for prizes, and the usual equipment therefor;

Theatrical scenery, properties, and apparel brought into the United States by proprietors or managers of theatrical exhibitions arriving from abroad for temporary use by them in such exhibitions;

Works of the free fine arts, drawings, engravings, photographic pictures, and philosophical and scientific apparatus brought into the United States by professional artists, lecturers, or scientists arriving from abroad for use by them for exhibition and in illustration, promotion, and encouragement of art, science, or industry in the United States.

Tea Admitted Free of Duty under Bond

Tea, tea waste, and tea siftings and sweepings, all the foregoing to be used solely for manufacturing theine, caffeine, or other chemical products whereby the identity and character of the original material is entirely destroyed or changed are free of duty under bond.

Personal Exemptions: Articles Admitted Free of Duty

Artificial limbs and limb braces imported solely for the personal use of a specified person and not for sale otherwise than for the use of such person;

Books, music, and pamphlets, in raised print for the blind used exclusively by or for them; Braille tablets, cubarithms, and special apparatus, machines, presses, and types for their use or benefit exclusively;

Articles of metal (including medals, trophies, and prizes), for bestowal on persons in the United States, as honorary distinctions, by foreign countries or citizens of foreign countries.

Upon request of the Department of State, articles from citizens of foreign countries for presentation to the president or vice president of the United States.

Chapter 14

APPRAISEMENT OF MERCHANDISE

Determining Factors

The Customs Simplification Act of 1956 adds a new valuation section to the United States Tariff Act of 1930, as amended. This new section is designated "Sec. 402. Value," and was effective February 27, 1958.

The old valuation section of the Tariff Act of 1930 is redesignated as "Sec. 402a. Value (Alternative)," and will continue to apply to the appraisement of all articles specified in the final list. The final list will not be subject to any change whatsoever by administrative action unless Congress passes some other legislation to change the situation. (See Imported Articles on the Official Final List, pages 82-83.)

The new valuation Sec. 402 applies to the appraisement of all imported articles not described on the final list.

Sec. 402a. Value (Alternative)

Basis. For the purposes of this act the value of imported merchandise shall be--

1. The foreign value or the export value, whichever is higher;

2. If the district or port director determines that neither the foreign value nor the export value can be satisfactorily ascertained, then the United States value;

3. If the district or port director determines that neither the foreign value, the export value, nor the United States value can be satisfactorily ascertained, then the cost of production;

4. In the case of an article with respect to which there is in effect a rate of duty based upon the American selling price of a domestic article, then the American selling price of such article.

Review of district or port director's decision. A decision of the district or port director that foreign value, export value, or United States value can not be satisfactorily ascertained shall be subject to review in reappraisement proceedings; but in any such proceeding, an affidavit executed outside of the United States shall not be admitted in evidence if executed by any person who fails to permit a treasury attaché to inspect his books, papers, records, accounts, documents, or correspondence, pertaining to the value or classification of such merchandise.

Foreign value. The foreign value of imported merchandise shall be the market value or the price at the time of exportation of such merchandise to the United States, at which such or similar merchandise is freely offered for sale for home consumption to all purchasers in the principal markets of the country from which exported, in the usual wholesale quantities and in the ordinary course of trade, including the cost of all containers and coverings of whatever nature, and all other costs, charges, and expenses incident to placing the merchandise in condition, packed ready for shipment to the United States.

Export value. The export value of imported merchandise shall be the market value or the price at the time of exportation of such merchandise to the United States, at which such or similar merchandise is freely offered for sale to all purchasers in the principal markets of the country from which exported, in the usual wholesale quantities and in the ordinary course of trade, for exportation to the United States, plus, when not included in such price, the cost of all containers and coverings of whatever nature, and all other costs, charges, and expenses incident to placing the merchandise in condition, packed ready for shipment to the United States.

United States value. The United States value of imported merchandise shall be the price at which such or similar imported merchandise is freely offered for sale for domestic consumption, packed ready for delivery, in the principal market of the United States to all purchasers, at the time of exportation of the imported merchandise, in the usual wholesale quantities and in the ordinary course of trade, with allowance made for duty, cost of transportation and insurance, and other necessary expenses from the place of shipment to the place of delivery, a commission not exceeding 6 percent, if any has been paid or contracted to be paid on goods secured otherwise than by purchase, or profits not to exceed 8 percent and a reasonable allowance for general expenses, not to exceed 8 percent on purchased goods.

Cost of production. For the purpose of this title the cost of production of imported merchandise shall be the sum of--

1. The cost of materials of, and of fabrication, manipulation, or other process employed in manufacturing or producing such or similar merchandise, at a time preceding the date of exportation of the particular merchandise under consideration which would ordinarily permit the manufacture or production of the particular merchandise under consideration in the usual course of business;

2. The usual general expenses (not less than 10 percent of such cost) in the case of such or similar merchandise;

3. The cost of all containers and coverings of whatever nature, and all other costs, charges, and expenses incident to placing the particular merchandise under consideration in condition, packed ready for shipment to the United States; and

4. An addition for profit (not less than 8 percent of the sum of the amounts found under paragraphs (1) and (2) of this subdivision) equal to the profit which ordinarily is added in the case of merchandise of the same general character as the particular merchandise under consideration, by manufacturers or producers in the country of manufacture or production who are engaged in the production or manufacture of merchandise of the same class or kind.

American selling price. The American selling price of any article manufactured or produced in the United States shall be the price, including the cost of all containers and coverings of whatever nature and all other costs, charges, and expenses incident to placing the merchandise in condition packed ready for delivery, at which such article is freely offered for sale for domestic consumption to all purchasers in the principal market of the United States, in the ordinary course of trade and in the usual wholesale quantities in such market, or the price that the manufacturer, producer, or owner would have received or was willing to receive for such merchandise when sold for domestic consumption in the ordinary course of trade and in the usual wholesale quantities, at the time of exportation of the imported article.

Sec. 402 Value

Basis. Except as otherwise specifically provided for in this act, the value of imported merchandise for the purposes of this act shall be--

1. the export value, or

2. if the export value cannot be determined satisfactorily, then the United States value, or

3. if neither the export value nor the United States value can be determined satisfactorily, then the constructed value; except that, in the case of an imported article subject to a rate of duty based on the American selling price of a domestic article, such value shall be--

4. the American selling price of such domestic article.

Export value. For the purposes of this section, the export value of imported merchandise shall be the price, at the time of exportation to the United States of the merchandise undergoing appraisement, at which such or similar merchandise is freely sold or, in the absence of sales, offered for sale in the principal markets of the country of exportation, in the usual wholesale quantities and in the ordinary course of trade, for exportation to the United States, plus, when not included in such price, the cost of all containers and coverings of whatever nature and all other expenses incidental to placing the merchandise in condition, packed ready for shipment to the United States.

United States value. For the purposes of this section, the United States value of imported merchandise shall be the price, at the time of exportation to the United States of the merchandise undergoing appraisement, at which such or similar merchandise is freely sold or, in the absence of sales, offered for sale in the principal market of the United States for domestic consumption, packed ready for delivery, in the usual wholesale quantities and in the ordinary course of trade, with allowances made for--

1. any commission usually paid or agreed to be paid, or the addition for profit and general expenses usually made, in connection with sales in such market of imported merchandise of the same class or kind as the merchandise undergoing appraisement;

2. the usual costs of transportation and insurance and other usual expenses incurred with respect to such or similar merchandise from the place of shipment to the place of delivery, not including any expense provided for in subdivision (1); and

3. the ordinary customs duties and other federal taxes currently payable on such or similar merchandise by reason of its importation, and any federal excise taxes on, or measured by the value of, such or similar merchandise, for which vendors

at wholesale in the United States are ordinarily liable.

If such or similar merchandise was not so sold or offered at the time of exportation of the merchandise undergoing appraisement, the United States value shall be determined, subject to the foregoing specifications of this subsection, from the price at which such or similar merchandise is so sold or offered at the earliest date after such time of exportation but before the expiration of ninety days after the importation of the merchandise undergoing appraisement.

Constructed value. For the purposes of this section, the constructed value of imported merchandise shall be the sum of--

1. the cost of materials (exclusive of any internal tax applicable in the country of exportation directly to such materials or their disposition, but remitted or refunded upon the exportation of the article in the production of which such materials are used) and of fabrication or other processing of any kind employed in producing such or similar merchandise, at a time preceding the date of exportation of the merchandise undergoing appraisement which would ordinarily permit the production of that particular merchandise in the ordinary course of business;

2. an amount for general expenses and profit equal to that usually reflected in sales of merchandise of the same general class or kind as the merchandise undergoing appraisement which are made by producers in the country of exportation, in the usual wholesale quantities and in the ordinary course of trade, for shipment to the United States; and

3. the cost of all containers and coverings of whatever nature, and all other expenses incidental to placing the merchandise undergoing appraisement in condition, packed ready for shipment to the United States.

American selling price. For the purposes of this section, the American selling price of any article produced in the United States shall be the price, including the cost of all containers and coverings of whatever nature and all other expenses incidental to placing the article in condition packed ready for delivery, at which such article is freely sold or, in the absence of sales, offered for sale for domestic consumption in the principal market of the United States, in the ordinary course of trade and in the usual wholesale quantities, or the price that the manufacturer, producer, or owner would have received or was willing to receive for such article when sold for domestic consumption in the ordinary course of trade and in the usual wholesale quantities, at the time of exportation of the imported article.

Transactions between related parties. The element of value is to be considered if the amount does not fairly reflect the sales in the market of merchandise of the same general class or kind as the merchandise going under appraisement and is not an arm length transaction, particularly in these instances:

1. members of a family, including brothers and sisters (whether by the whole or half blood), spouse, ancestors, and lineal descendants;

2. any officer or director of an organization and such organization;

3. partners;

4. employer and employee;

5. any person directly or indirectly owning, controlling, or holding with power to vote, 5 percent or more of the outstanding voting stock or shares of any organization and such organization; and

6. two or more persons directly or indirectly controlling, controlled by, or under common control with, any person.

When merchandise is appraised in Sec. 402 new law, the import specialist is authorized not only to ascertain at which prices such or similar merchandise is sold for home consumption in the country of exportation but he can also compare values from third countries as well in order to determine appraised value.

The basic purpose is to determine relationships between buyer and seller, particularly when a foreign exporter sells goods to an importer, and is a wholly owned subsidiary, and all the profits to accrue in the United States on the resale of the merchandise. This applies when a lower price is shown on the invoice whereas the same or similar merchandise is sold to persons not related at a higher price.

Some Differences Between Sec. 402a and Sec. 402 of the Tariff Act of 1930, as Amended

Wholesale quantities refer to those quantities in which the largest number of transactions occur rather than how small the aggregate of such quantities is in relation to the total volume sold. To illustrate:

Number of sales	Quantity	Aggregate Volume	Sales Price
100	150 dz.	15,000 dz.	$3.50 per dz.
150	85 dz.	12,750 dz.	$3.75 per dz.
200	50 dz.	10,000 dz.	$4.00 per dz.

Under the old law Sec. 402a, the usual wholesale quantity is the largest number of individual transactions, such as 200 sales in 50 dz. lots and the dutiable value would be $4.00 per dz.

Under the new law Sec. 402, the usual wholesale quantity is the quantity in which the greatest aggregate volume is sold, which is 15,000 dz. in 150 dz. lots and the dutiable value would be $3.50 per dz.

Export value. Under export value Sec. 402a, there is a difference in export value compared to Sec. 402. Under Sec. 402a, the language of the tariff speaks of selling merchandise freely to all purchasers in the ordinary course of trade in the usual wholesale quantities rather than at wholesale or selected purchasers.

Under Sec. 402, new law, the language is at a variance with Sec. 402a in that the term "freely sold, or in the absence of sales, offered for sale" applies

1. to all purchasers at wholesale or

2. in the ordinary course of trade to one or more selected purchasers at wholesale at a price which fairly reflects the market value of the merchandise.

The new valuation permits the usage for transactions including exclusive selling agents and representatives.

United States value. Under Sec. 402a, the definition states "a commission not exceeding 6 per centum if any has been paid or contracted to be paid." Sec. 402 states "any commission usually paid or agreed to be paid." Sec. 402a states "8 per centum for profit and 8 per centum for general expenses" for purchased merchandise. Under Sec. 402 as for profit and general expenses, the addition for profit and general expenses is the amount that is usually made in connection with sales in such market of imported merchandise of the same class or kind as the merchandise undergoing appraisement.

Under Sec. 402, additional factors have been included.

1. The ordinary customs duties and other federal

taxes currently payable on such or similar merchandise by reason of its importation and any federal excise taxes, or measured by the value of such or similar merchandise, for which vendors at wholesale in the United States are ordinarily liable.

2. If such or similar merchandise was not sold or offered at the time of exportation of the merchandise undergoing appraisement, the United States value shall be determined from the price at which such or similar merchandise is sold or offered at the earliest date after such time of exportation but before the expiration of ninety days after the importation in the country of exportation, in the usual wholesale quantities and in the ordinary course of trade for shipment to the United States.

Under Sec. 402a allowance for profit and overhead of 8 percent for each on purchased merchandise is made, whereas, under Sec. 402 deductions will be mark up for profit and general expenses usually made by the largest segment of the import trade in connection with the sale of the import articles of the same class or kind as the article undergoing appraisement.

On consigned merchandise, where the importer under Sec. 402a received a commission not exceeding 6 percent, under Sec. 402 (new law) the deduction will be the commission paid or agreed to be paid to importers of the same class or kind of goods.

Cost of production Sec. 402a. Variance is as follows with Sec. 402.

1. The category under Sec. 402 is known as constructed value.

2. The cost of materials (exclusive of any internal tax applicable in the country of exportation directly to such materials or their disposition but remitted or refunded upon the exportation of the article in the production of which such materials are used).

3. An amount for general expenses and profit equal to that usually reflected in sales of merchandise of the same general class or kind as the merchandise undergoing appraisement which are made by producers.

American selling price. Under Sec. 402 (new law), the term "freely sold or, in the absence of sales, offers for sale" is limited to all purchasers at wholesale, in the ordinary course of trade to one or more selected purchasers at wholesale at a price which fairly reflects the market value of the merchandise.

The valuation difference between Sec. 402a Final List and Sec. 402 is that under Sec. 402 sales have precedence over offers for sale by domestic manufacturers to their customers in the United States, but in the absence of such sales or offers resort must be made to the price that the American manufacturer, producer, or owner would have received or was willing to receive for his merchandise when sold for consumption in the United States at the time the imported article was exported from abroad.

In the ordinary course of trade, the domestic article is sold only to wholesalers or retailers, the price to the wholesaler will be used for appraisement purposes.,

Under Sec. 402a, sales or offers to exclusive agents are not considered because the goods are not freely offered for sale to all purchasers at wholesale.

Under Sec. 402, priority will be given to sales made to purchasers in the usual wholesale quantities either for industrial use or for resale at wholesale. Sales to retailers will only be considered when there are no sales or offers to wholesalers or to industrial users.

IMPORTED ARTICLES SPECIFIED ON THE OFFICIAL FINAL LIST

Chemicals, Oils and Paints
Coal-Tar Products: Colors, Dyes, Stains, Color Acids, Bases, and Similar Products; Intermediates; Medicinals; Other Finished Products.

Non-Coal-Tar Drugs and Medicinals: Industrial Chemicals.

Medicinal and Pharmaceutical Preparations

Miscellaneous Products
Extracts and flavoring, gelatins, glues, inks, polishes, and tapes, etc.

Oils, Distilled or Essential

Pigments, Paints and Varnishes

Soap and Toilet Preparations

Earths, Earthenware and Glassware
Earthenware, earthy or mineral substances or articles; glassware; optical goods.

Metals and Manufactures of
Bearings and parts, ball and roller; bullions, metal threads, lame or lahn, and articles made therefrom; electric articles and parts other than machinery; household, kitchen, and table utensils; knives, including machine knives and cutlery; machines, machinery and parts thereof.

Mill Products: aluminum; nickel; steel.

Miscellaneous Metal Articles: Needles; scientific, laboratory, and professional apparatus, instruments, and equipment; tools and gauges; vehicles; vessels and parts.

82

Wood and Manufactures of
Sugar, Molasses, and Manufactures of
Agricultural Products and Provisions
Baked articles; dairy products; fruits and preparations; fodders and feeds; meat products; miscellaneous edible preparations; nursery and greenhouse stock.

Cotton Manufactures
Flax, Hemp, Jute and Manufactures of
Wool and Manufactures of
Silk Manufactures
Manufactures of Rayon and Other Synthetic Textiles
Paper and Books
Books and other printed matter, papers; board products; miscellaneous paper articles.

Sundries
Cameras and photographic supplies; furs and manufactures; leather and manufactures; miscellaneous articles; musical instruments or articles; ornamented or embroidered fabrics and articles, and laces, nets, and veilings; rubber articles; sporting and fishing equipment.

Note: Imported merchandise not listed on the Final List will not be appraised on Foreign Value (there is no comparable provision under Sec. 402).

It is impossible to enumerate the number of items included in each specific category.

Should you desire further information it is suggested that you contact the District Director or Regional Commissioner of the Port of New York of the U.S. Customs Service.

Chapter 15

MARKING: COUNTRY OF ORIGIN

Merchandise Exempt From Marking

The following need not be marked with the country of origin:

1. Articles imported by mail for the personal use of the importer or tourist and not intended for sale in their imported condition.

2. Articles that are incapable of being marked.

3. Articles that cannot be marked prior to shipment to the United States without injury.

4. Articles that cannot be marked prior to shipment to the United States except at an expense economically prohibitive of their importation.

5. Crude substances.

6. Articles produced more than twenty years prior to their importation into the United States.

Although such articles are exempt from marking to indicate the country of origin, the outermost containers in which such articles will ordinarily reach the ultimate purchaser in the United States must be marked to show the country of origin of such articles.

7. When the marking of the container of an article will reasonably indicate the country of origin of the article, the article itself is exempt from such marking. This applies only when the article will reach the ultimate purchaser in an unopened container (sealed container).

8. An article that is to be processed in the United States by the importer or his account otherwise than for the purpose of concealing the origin of such article, and in such manner that any mark of origin would necessarily be obliterated, destroyed or permanently concealed.

9. An article with respect to which an ultimate purchaser in the United States, by reason of the character of the article, must necessarily know the country of origin even though the article is not marked to indicate its origin.

Marking Requirements Under Sec. 304 Of The Tariff Act
Of 1930, As Amended

Imported articles must be marked legibly and indelibly in the English language, with few exceptions, and in a conspicuous place, as will indicate to the ultimate purchaser in the United States the name of the country of origin of the merchandise.

The country of manufacture or production shall be considered the country of origin. Further work or material added to the article in another country must effect a substantial transformation in order to render such other country the "country of origin."

The term "country" as used in this section of the tariff act requires the marking of articles to indicate country of origin and shall be considered to mean the political entity known as a nation.

U. S. Customs deems it sufficient if at the time of examination the marking of the country of origin remains on the article to indicate evidence of permanency.

Imported merchandise that will be substantially changed in the United States, so that the articles in their changed condition will become products of the United States, need not have any additional words as to foreign origin to indicate where each article was manufactured.

If an article (or its container when the container and not the article must be marked) is not properly marked at the time of importation, a marking duty equal to 10 percent of the customs value will be assessed unless the article is exported, destroyed, or properly marked under customs supervision. (The importer does not have the option of paying a special marking duty of 10 percent in lieu of marking the merchandise.)

When an imported article is combined with another article after importation, but before delivery to an ultimate purchaser, and the name indicating the country of origin of the article appears in a place on the article so that the name of the article will be visible after combining, the marking shall include, in addition to the name of the country of origin, words or symbols that shall clearly show that the origin indicated is that of the imported article only and not that of any other article with which the imported article may be combined after importation. If empty drums or bottles or other containers that are imported into the United States are to be filled with another article in the United States, they should be marked to show the country of origin of the drum, bottle, or other container, e.g., "made in France."

Containers bearing a United States address of imported merchandise, bearing the name and address of the importer or distributor or of a company in the United States, shall be marked in close proximity to the United States address to indicate country of origin of the contents with a marking "contents made in England."

Special Marking Requirements

Articles such as knives, clippers, shears, safety razors, pincers and parts thereof, and vacuum containers or parts thereof, shall be marked legibly and conspicuously, in the English language, to indicate country of origin by die stamping, cast in the mold lettering, etching (acid or electrolytic), engraving, or by means of metal plates that bear the necessary marking and that are securely attached to the article in a conspicuous place by welding, screws, or rivets.

Any inquiries concerning metal articles as to country of origin should be addressed to the district or port director of customs at the closest port.

Chapter 16

PROHIBITED AND RESTRICTED MERCHANDISE

Automobile Safety Standards

All imported automobiles or automobile equipment, whether new or used, manufactured after December 31, 1967 (except those designed for competition, show, test or experimental purposes), will be refused entry into the United States unless they are in conformity with applicable federal motor vehicle safety standards. An imported automobile or automobile equipment that is intended solely for exportation and is so labeled is exempt from these safety standards.

Automobile Emission Standards

The federal law dealing with air pollution control prohibits the importation into the United States of any motor vehicle not certified as meeting applicable emission standards.

In general, emission standards apply to all passenger cars and light trucks, beginning with the 1968 model. Such vehicles are subject to crankcase and exhaust emission standards and, beginning with the 1971 model, fuel evaporative standards. Vehicles with an engine that has a displacement of less than fifty cubic inches are subject only to the crankcase emission standard until the 1973 model, when they are subject to exhaust and evaporative emission standards as well.

Motorcycles are not subject to emission standards. For imported vehicles, these standards apply whether the vehicle is new or used. They now apply to vehicles imported for personal use as well as those imported for sale or resale. Vehicles imported for display, competition, and testing are not required to conform to emission standards, provided they are not sold or licensed for use on the public roads.

Wild or Game Animals, Birds, Fish, Amphibians, Reptiles, Mollusks, Crustaceans, and Parts or Products Thereof; Prohibited and Endangered Species

The importation of live wild or game animals, birds, and

other wildlife, or any part or product made therefrom, and the eggs of wild or game birds, is subject to certain prohibitions, restrictions, permit and quarantine requirements of several government departments. Importations of wildlife, parts, or products thereof, are subject to the requirements of customs entry at certain designated ports of entry.

Endangered species of wildlife and certain species of animals and birds prohibited entry into the United States may be imported only under license or permit granted by the Bureau of Sport Fisheries and Wildlife, Department of the Interior, Washington, D. C. 20240. Specific information concerning import requirements should be obtained from that agency or, in the case of marine mammals, from the National Marine Fisheries Service, Department of Commerce, Washington, D. C. 20235.

The importation into the United States of any wild animal or bird is prohibited if such animal or bird was captured, taken, shipped, possessed, or exported contrary to the law of the foreign country or subdivision thereof. In addition, no wild animal or bird from any foreign country may be taken, purchased, sold, or possessed contrary to the laws of any state, territory or possession of the United States.

The importation of the feathers or skin of any wild bird, except for scientific and educational purposes, is prohibited. This prohibition does not apply to fully-manufactured artificial flies used for fishing.

The feathers of certain birds for use in the manufacture of artificial flies used for fishing or for millinery purposes may be imported under permit issued by the Secretary of the Interior, Washington, D. C. 20240.

Live birds protected under the Migratory Bird Treaty Act may be imported into the United States from foreign countries for scientific or propagating purposes only under permits issued by the Bureau of Sport Fisheries and Wildlife, U. S. Department of Interior, Washington, D. C. 20240. Such migratory birds and certain game mammals (antelope, mountain sheep, deer, bears, peccaries, squirrels, rabbits, and hares) imported from Mexico, must be accompanied by Mexican export permits.

Importations in this class are also subject to the quarantine requirements of the Department of Agriculture and the United States Public Health Service, Department of Health, Education, and Welfare. Appropriate inquiries in this respect should be directed to those agencies also.

Wildlife is defined as any wild mammal, wild bird, amphibian, reptile, mollusk or crustacean, or any part, product, egg and offspring thereof, or the dead body or parts thereof whether or not included in a manufactured product.

Fish for the purpose of these regulations is defined as any finfish or any part, product, egg or offspring thereof, or the dead body or parts thereof whether or not included in a manufactured product.

An export permit or other document from an appropriate government official in English, or the original document and a certified translation thereof, from each country where the fish or wildlife is subject to regulations regarding its taking, transportation, or sale, that shows that such fish or wildlife was lawfully taken, transported or sold, or a consular certificate from an American consul that shows that an appropriate government officer has certified to the consul the information required.

Fish or wildlife on the endangered species list cannot be exported from this country unless accompanied by a permit issued by the Department of the Interior, Bureau of Sport Fisheries and Wildlife.

Any importation entering this country contrary to law may be subject to seizure and forfeiture and the portion involved subject to civil and criminal penalties.

Biological Materials

The importation into the United States for sale, barter, or exchange of any virus, therapeutic serum, toxin, antitoxin, or analogous products, or arsphenamine or its derivatives (or any other trivalent organic arsenic compound) applicable to the prevention, treatment, or cure of diseases or injuries of man is prohibited unless such products have been propagated or prepared at an establishment holding an unsuspended and unrevoked license for such manufacturing issued by the Secretary, Department of Health, Education, and Welfare. Samples of the licensed product must accompany each importation for forwarding by the port director of customs, at the port of entry, to the Director, Division of Biologics Standards, National Institutes of Health, Bethesda, Maryland.

A permit from the U.S. Public Health Service is required for shipments of causative organisms or transmitting agents of human disease.

Rags

Rags and similar material presented for importation into the United States are subject to foreign quarantine regulations of the U.S. Public Health Service. If the quarantine officer at the port of arrival has reason to believe that the material might otherwise be infected with certain communicable disease, he may require certificates of disinfection before release of imported material will be permitted by customs; or if such a certificate is not presented within a reasonable time, he may require the material to be disinfected in a manner satisfactory to the quarantine officer at the expense of the importer, or to be exported or disposed of as directed by the U.S. Public Health Service.

Brushes

Shipments of lather brushes made from animal hair or bristles are governed by foreign quarantine regulations of the U.S. Public Health Service.

Other prohibited or restricted importations include any merchandise found to be in unfair competition, white or yellow phosphorus matches, pepper shells, switchblade knives, and commodities subject to import quotas or restrained to specified levels under bilateral or multilateral trade agreements or arrangements.

Since all restrictions and prohibitions are subject to change under the laws and regulations by which they are controlled, the foreign shipper and the prospective importer may save time and money by securing proper information beforehand from the agency that administers the particular laws and regulations applicable to the proposed importation.

Alcoholic Beverages and Confectionery

Alcoholic beverages are nonmailable with certain exceptions and when imported in the mails are subject to seizure and forfeiture. The addressee shall be advised that they are subject to forfeiture and that he has a right to file a petition for their release.

Conditions for release: If the district director of customs is satisfied that there was no fraudulent intent involved, he may release the alcoholic beverages to the addressee upon the following conditions:

1. Applicable duty and internal revenue tax shall be paid.
2. The addressee shall comply with the alcoholic beverage laws of the state to which the shipment is destined.
3. Any other conditions the district director may impose under his authority to remit or mitigate fines, penalties and forfeitures shall be complied with.
4. The addressee, his representative, or a common carrier shall pick up the merchandise at the customs office where it is being held.

Since the merchandise is nonmailable, it cannot be delivered at the post office.

Confectionery that bears or contains any alcohol is prohibited, except that this does not apply to any confectionery by reason of its containing less than .5 percent by volume of alcohol derived solely from the use of flavoring extracts.

Arms, Ammunition, Explosives and Implements of War

To import arms, ammunition, or any implements of war, it is essential to obtain a license that is issued by the Department of State, Bureau of Alcohol, Tobacco and Firearms (ATF), Department of the Treasury. There must be compliance with the international traffic arms regulations of the department. Applications to import are extended to licensed importers, dealers, or manufacturers.

The exception to the general rule is that for firearms or ammunitions that were previously taken out of the United States and registered at any U.S. Customhouse or ATF field office before leaving for abroad, no import permit is necessary. This will facilitate returning to the United States without any difficulty. The quantity, however, is limited in that three nonautomatic firearms and 1,000 cartridges may be registered for one person only.

Specific inquiries should be addressed to the Office of Munitions Control, Department of State, Washington, D.C. 20520.

Counterfeit Coins, Currencies, Stamps, and Securities

In accordance with chapter 25 of the U.S. Code, any token, disk, or device in the likeness or similtude of any coin of the United States or a foreign country, counterfeits of coins in circulation in the United States, counterfeited, forged or altered obligations or other securities of the United States or of any foreign government, or plates, dies or other apparatus that may be used in making any of the foregoing, when brought into the United States shall be seized and delivered to the nearest representatives of the U.S. Secret Service.

Printed matter containing illustrations or reproductions of colored postage stamps (uncancelled) if the size is less than 3/4 or more than 1-1/2 inches is permissible. Black and white facsimile of cancelled postage stamps are also permissible.

Foreign Assets Control Regulations

The control of all financial and commercial transactions involving Cuba or nationals thereof, including North Korea, North Vietnam, and Rhodesia is under the direction of the Foreign Assets Control.

The secretary of the treasury by means of regulations, rulings, licenses, or otherwise deals or engages in any transaction with respect to any merchandise outside the United States if such merchandise is of

1. Cuban origin or
2. Is or has been located in or transported from or through Cuba or
3. Is made, or derived in whole or in part of any article that is the growth, produce or manufacture of Cuba.

Importations of merchandise of Rhodesia, North Korea, North Vietnam, are not licensed. However, certain specified commodities are permitted if sufficient proof is submitted relative thereto. Customs requires certificates or licenses for the importation of merchandise from Rhodesia. Items not in compliance with the regulations shall be detained and seized.

The Foreign Assets Control will issue licenses to allow certain commodities when certified to be of countries other than stated herein, in which they are produced and from which they are exported.

Goods of mainland China are now authorized to be imported under general licenses contained in the regulations. All goods originating in mainland China are subject to the statutory rates of duty in the tariff applicable to communist countries even though the merchandise was purchased through and shipped from another country, i.e., South Korea, Japan, or Hong Kong. The determining factor is where the merchandise was produced. If produced in any of these three countries, the regular rate of duty would apply.

The supplier of the merchandise should certify on the commercial invoice where the merchandise was manufactured. Should there be a concealment or a misrepresentation of this fact, the importer could be subject to a severe penalty under Sec. 1592 of the U.S. Code or Sec. 592 of the tariff act.

The Trade Act of 1974 denies the treatment of benefits of trade or credit to communist countries that restrict emigration. Should this issue be overcome, the president would be authorized to enter into bilateral agreements for three-year periods with these countries, subject to a renewal for an additional period if trade negotiations are favorable.

Fruits, Plants, Plant Products, Insects, and Insecticides

Plants and plant products include fruits and vegetables, nursery stock, bulbs, roots, cut flowers, etc.

The importation into the United States of plants and plant products is subject to the rules and regulations of the Department of Agriculture. At the time of importation the customs officer inspects the commodities and ascertains if an inspection certificate has been issued. A permit issued by the Plant Quarantine Division is required.

Live insects that are injurious to crops are prohibited except when imported for scientific purposes by the secretary of agriculture or when not injurious to crops if a permit is issued by the Plant Quarantine Division.

Insecticides, Paris green, fungicides, and herbicides are governed by the Pesticides Regulation Division, Environmental Protection Agency, Washington, D.C., 20460.

Livestock, Meat, and Meat-food Products

All meat and meat-food products offered for entry into the United States are subject to the regulations prescribed by the Secretary of agriculture and shall not be released from customs custody prior to inspection by an inspector of the Animal and Plant Health Inspection Service, except when authority is given by such inspector for inspection at the importer's premises or other place not under customs supervision.

Importation of the following are subject to inspection and quarantine regulations: All cloven-hoofed animals (except from Canada and certain northern states of Mexico), meat from such animals, meat-food products, including the various varieties of wild hog, live poultry (except from Canada), dressed poultry and eggs thereof for hatching, animal by-products, horse meat and horse-meat products. However, the importation of cloven-hoofed animals and their meat products from any country where rinderpest or foot-and-mouth disease exists is prohibited.

For a foreign meat inspection, it is essential that a certificate from the supplier of the country of origin be submitted prior to the time of examination.

Foreign cured meats also require proper certification from the foreign supplier to be approved by the Department of Agriculture.

Hay and straw packing material from any country where rinderpest or foot-and-mouth disease exists is prohibited unless accompanied by an appropriate certificate of an American consular officer that such material has been disinfected in compliance with the regulations of the Department of Agriculture.

Narcotic Drugs and Derivatives

The importation of narcotics, marihuana, and other dangerous drugs is prohibited except when imported in compliance with regulations promulgated by the attorney general. Examples of some of the prohibited narcotic drugs follow.

Amphetamines are mostly known to the public as benzedrine, which acts directly on the central nervous system.

Barbiturates are derived from barbituric acids veronal and luminal. They are extremely valuable compounds that, by their action on the higher centers of the brain, bring on sleep. They are also used as anesthetics and to a limited extent in the method of psychoanalysis.

Like the opiates, the barbiturates calm and sooth and are for this reason liable to be abused by neurotic individuals who take them first on medical advice as aids to sleep and later continue to take them in increasing amounts until addiction results.

Coca leaves and derivatives such as cocaine. Similar to benzedrine in its effects is another much-abused drug, cocaine. The plant from which this substance is obtained was endowed with divine properties by the people of Peru. The habit of chewing coca leaves is still widespread among the poorer Indians of Peru. The modern trend is to take the purified alkaloid cocaine and inject it into the blood stream by means of a hypodermic syringe. Cocaine is a stimulant that acts first on the higher levels of the brain. It is very destructive to health and definitely leads to criminal and violent acts.

Mescaline (Peyote) is derived from the buttons of a cactus plant. It belongs to the large and important groups of chemicals known as amines, many of which have a powerful action on the chemistry of the body, e.g., adrenalin. Those who have taken the drug show the physical symptoms of restlessness, tremor, weakness, sweating and mental and emotional changes.

Marihuana and other forms of cannabis are derivatives from the Indian hemp plant Cannabis sativa. It is a tall gangling weed that may reach a height of ten feet. Marihuana means all parts of the plant, whether growing or not, the seeds thereof, the resin extracted and every compound, manufacture, salt, derivative, mixture, etc. It grows in Mexico, Africa, the Middle East, and India and can be smoked in short cigarettes. Hashish is a derivative of this plant.

Opium is a product of the opium poppy (Papaver somniferum). The opium poppy will grow in many climates, but its cultivation for the purpose of opium manufacture is confined to a few countries, e.g., India, Iran, Turkey, Yugoslavia, Macedonia, and China. The brownish gum is extremely rich in alkaloids, morphine, codeine, and papaverine. It is manufactured from morphine by a relatively simple chemical procedure and is known chemically as diacetyl-morphine. Its manufacture is prohibited in the United States.

Products of Convict or Forced Labor

The importation is prohibited of merchandise produced, mined, or manufactured by means of the use of convict labor, forced labor, or indentured labor under penal sections.

Milk

The importation into the United States of milk and cream is prohibited unless the person by whom such milk or cream is shipped or tranported into the United States holds a valid permit from the Public Health Service. Permitted importations of milk and cream must meet all requirements prescribed by the Public Health Service, Department of Health and Welfare as to the labeling and marking.

Photographic Films

All imported photographic films that accompany the traveler, if not for commercial purposes, may be released without examination by a customs officer unless there is reason to believe that they contain objectionable matter.

Films prohibited for entry are those that contain obscene matter, advocating treason or insurrection against the United States, or advocating forcible resistance to any law of the United States, or those that threaten the life or infliction of bodily harm upon any person in the United States.

Nuclear Reactors and Radioactive Materials

All forms of thorium, plutonium, and uranium, including many radioisotopes and all nuclear reactors imported into the United States, are subject to the provisions of regulations of the U.S. Atomic Energy Commission in addition to import regulations imposed by any other agency of the United States. Authority to import these commodities is controlled by the Atomic Energy Commission.

Information concerning the Atomic Energy Commission import requirements may be obtained from the U.S. Atomic Energy Commission, Washington, D.C., 20545.

Eggs and Egg Products

Noncommercial importations of eggs and egg products may be released upon oral declaration that they are imported exclusively for the importer's personal use, display or laboratory analysis and not for sale or distribution.

Importation of commercial quantities of shell eggs (domesticated chicken, duck, goose, poultry or guinea fowl) and egg products (including dried, liquid or frozen products) are subject to restrictions and may not be released from customs custody prior to approval by the Poultry Division, Agricultural Marketing Service, U.S. Department of Agriculture,

Washington, D. C. 20250. This requirement does not apply to importation of fresh eggs in the shell.

Importations of eggs, including eggs for hatching, from a foreign country shall be accompanied by a certificate signed by a veterinary officer of the country of origin certifying that the eggs were washed, sanitized, and packed according to the regulations of the Animal and Plant Health Inspection Services and produced by flocks known to be free of Newcastle disease.

The eggs of certain birds are also restricted, such as eggs of migratory kinds of ducks, geese, pigeons, and doves. Exceptions may be made for shipments imported for scientific, educational or research purposes.

Teas

The regular importation of tea that is inferior in purity, quality, and fitness for consumption is prohibited. It is subject to the provisions of the Federal Food, Drug and Cosmetic Act and regulations thereunder. However, tea for personal use, when imported in a passenger's baggage, in one or more packages weighing not more than five pounds each, may be imported without examination for purity and without payment of the examination fee.

White Phosphorus Matches

The importation of such matches into the United States is prohibited. Invoices covering matches shall be accompanied by a certificate of official inspection of the government of the country of manufacture. In the absence of such certificates, the matches shall be detained until a certificate is produced or the importer submits satisfactory evidence to show that the matches were not in fact manufactured with the use of poisonous white or yellow phosphorus.

Antidumping Act

When the secretary of the treasury determines that a class or kind of imported merchandise is being or is likely to be sold to purchasers in the United States at less than its fair value, he shall advise the U. S. Tariff Commission, which shall determine whether an industry in the United States is being or is likely to be injured, or is prevented from being established, by reason of the importation of such merchandise. If the tariff commission's determination is in the affirmative, the secretary must make public a finding of dumping and the importation of the merchandise becomes subject to the assessment of dumping duties equal to the amount by which the foreign market value or constructed value exceeds the purchase price or exporter's sales price, as applicable.

The Trade Act of 1974 provides that amendments were made relative to antidumping. Its purpose was to speed up the process of the administration of the antidumping act. Within thirty days of the receipt of the complaint, the treasury must conduct a summary investigation. If the result indicates that the act may have been violated, the secretary of the treasury is directed to publish a notice whereby an invitation of a formal investigation will take place. He has six to nine months to do so, depending how involved the case may be. If he finds that the act has been violated, the withholding of the appraisement of the merchandise commences, and within three months from that date, the secretary must make a final determination whether or not the merchandise is being or likely to be sold in the United States at less than its fair value. If decided in the affirmative the case goes to the international trade commissioner for an injury determination.

Chapter 17

APPLIED LAW ENFORCEMENTS BY U. S. CUSTOMS SERVICE

Antismuggling Act

The provisions of law applying to the high seas adjacent to customs waters of the United States shall be enforced in a customs-enforcement area upon any vessel, merchandise, or person found therein.

The customs authority within that area may go on board any vessel and make a thorough examination, bring it into port, and based on the regulations of the secretary of the treasury, seize, arrest the unlawful introduction into or removal from the United States of any merchandise or person. The limitations are that no officer of the United States has the authority to enforce the law upon the high seas upon a foreign vessel in contravention of any treaty with a foreign government except as such authorities be permitted under special arrangement with such foreign government.

Whenever any vessel is employed to defend the revenue or to smuggle any merchandise into the United States, or to smuggle any merchandise in the territory of any foreign government in violation of the laws there in force, if under the laws of that foreign government any penalty or forfeiture is provided for violation of laws of the United States respecting customs revenue, or whenever any vessel shall be found to have been employed within the United States for any such purpose, if not subsequently forfeited to the United States or to a foreign government, and is found at any place at which any vessel may be examined by a customs officer in the enforcement of any law respecting the revenue, the vessel and its cargo shall be seized and forfeited.

Any vessel or vehicle forfeited to the United States, whether summarily or by a decree of any court, for violation of any law respecting the revenue, may, in the discretion of the secretary of the treasury, if he deems it necessary to protect the revenue of the United States, be destroyed in lieu of the sale thereof under existing law.

Controlled Substance Import and Export Act

It shall be unlawful for any person to bring or possess on board any vessel or aircraft, or any vehicle arriving in or departing from the United States, a controlled substance or narcotic drug unless such substance or drug is a part of the cargo entered on the manifest or part of the official supplies of the vessel, aircraft, or vehicle.

In July, 1973, a reorganization plan was based on an executive order that established the Drug Enforcement Administration in the Department of Justice for the enforcement of drug laws. This law empowered the attorney general to authorize the coordination of maximum cooperation between the Drug Enforcement Administration, the F.B.I., and other units of the Department of Justice to enforce the laws respecting narcotics and dangerous drugs.

A permit to import crude opium and coca leaves should be obtained from the Department of Justice, Bureau of Narcotics and Dangerous Drugs. These drugs may be imported for medical, scientific, or other legitimate purposes. Registration is necessary for such importations; however, the attorney general may suspend registration when he finds that there is an imminent danger of any drugs to the health and safety of the people.

No crude opium may be imported for the purpose of manufacturing heroin or smoking opium. Inquiries should be addressed to the Drug Enforcement Administration, Department of Justice, Washington, D. C. 20537.

Navigation Laws

Customs exercises functions provided for in the navigation laws pertaining to the entry and clearance of vessels in domestic trades, including fisheries.

Internal Revenue Code (Internal Revenue Service)

It is the U. S. Customs function to collect taxes on alcohol, tobacco, sugar, oleomargarine, cigars, cigarettes, medical preparations, perfumery, distilled wines, and malt liquor.

Cigars and cigarettes imported in the United States, except by mail and in baggage, shall be placed in a designated bonded warehouse to remain until inspected, weighed, and repacked, if necessary, under customs and Internal Revenue Laws.

American Goods Returned

The immediate containers of all domestic cigars, cigarettes, medicinal preparations, and perfumery that are returned to the United States and are subject to a duty equal to an Internal Revenue tax shall be stamped with the legend "U. S. Customs - American Goods Returned."

United States Criminal Code

The importation of any book, pamphlet, paper, writing, advertisement, circular, print, picture or drawing containing any matter advocating treason or insurrection against the United States, or forcible resistance to any law of the United States, or containing any threat to take the life of or inflict bodily harm upon any person in the United States, or any obscene matter or article, or any drug or medicine or any article for causing unlawful abortion, or any lottery ticket, or any printed paper that may be used as a lottery ticket, or any advertisement of any lottery is prohibited. No such articles, whether imported separately or contained in packages with other goods entitled to entry, shall be admitted to entry (the admissible goods will be separated from the unadmissible goods), provided that the prohibited articles were included without the knowledge or consent of the importer, owner, agent or consignee; otherwise the entire contents of the package shall be subject to seizure and forfeiture.

Any book or printed matter held by customs as a seizure shall await the judgment of the district court. Upon such seizure of such book or matter the customs officer shall transmit information thereof to the district attorney of the district in which such seizure was made, who shall institute proceedings in the district court for the forfeiture, confiscation, and destruction of the book or matter seized.

Upon the adjudication that such book or matter thus seized is of the character the entry of which is by this section prohibited, the book or matter shall be destroyed. Upon adjudication that such book or matter thus seized is not of such character, the book or matter shall not be excluded from entry under provision of this section.

In any such proceeding, any interested party may upon demand have the facts at issue determined by a jury and the party may have an appeal or the right of review as in the case of ordinary actions or suits.

Import Quotas

Various import quotas were established by legislation and presidential proclamations issued pursuant to specific legislation and are provided for in the tariff schedules of the United States and administered by the commissioner of customs and other government agencies.

Importation and Exportation of Gold (Department of Treasury)

Regarding gold, gold bullion, and gold medals, prior to the passage of Public Law 93-373 issued August 14, 1974, and effective December 31, 1974, the following was in force and effect:

The gold coins minted before 1934 were permitted entry without a license if they were collector's items only. Where jewelry contained gold coins the same rules applied.

Gold bullion was prohibited unless a license was obtained.

Only gold medals presented as awards were permissible, all others were prohibited.

At the present time no license is required for the importation of gold jewelry, bullion, or medals.

As for gold coins, or currency or other monetary instruments exceeding $5,000 in the aggregate amount, if shipped from the United States outside the country, or any place outside the United States into the United States, a report must be made to the Treasury Department on Department of the Treasury, Internal Revenue Service Form 4790. All restrictions on the purchase, holding, or selling of or otherwise dealing with gold were removed effective December 31, 1974.

Gold may be imported subject to the usual customs entry requirements. Importations of gold and silver coins in excess of $5,000 that are accepted and used as money in the country of issue are, however, subject to the requirements of the Currency and Foreign Transactions Reporting Act. Inquiries should be directed to the Office of Domestic

Gold and Silver Operations, Department of the Treasury, Washington, D. C. 20220.

Prosecution for Violation of the Customs Laws

When there is a seizure or other violation of the U. S. Customs laws requiring legal proceedings by civil or criminal action, the district director or special agent in charge of the area shall furnish a report to the United States attorney and action shall be taken accordingly.

Chapter 18

OPERATIONAL CONTROL WITH OTHER GOVERNMENT UNITS

Public Health Service: Importation of Birds, Monkeys, Dogs, Cats and Other Pets Subject to Foreign Quarantine Regulations

Birds may be imported (but not for trade or sale). However, not more than two birds in cages may be imported by the owner as pets, if the birds are known not to be affected with or exposed to any communicable disease of poultry. Pet birds must be entered only at specifically designated ports of entry and be examined by a U.S. Department of Agriculture Animal and Plant Health Inspection Service (APHIS) Veterinary Services veterinarian upon entry. A statement must be provided that the birds have been in the owner's possession for at least ninety days prior to entry and during that time have not been in contact with poultry or other birds; that the birds will be maintained in confinement in his personal possession apart from all other birds for at least thirty days; that the birds will be made available for health inspection on request; and that federal officials will be notified of any signs of disease or if a bird dies during that period.

A maximum of two disease-free psittacine birds, including parrots, cockatoos, macaws, and parakeets, may be imported by the owner as pets, but not for sale or trade, provided that neither he nor any member of his family within his household has imported any other psittacine bird in the preceding twelve months. Such birds may be imported only if they meet the above APHIS Veterinary Services requirements in addition to the Public Health Service Requirements. After arrival, all psittacine birds are to be treated by or under supervision of a licensed veterinarian as prescribed by regulations of the Public Health Service.

The purpose of control or restrictions of pets is to safeguard your health as well as to keep out of the country those animals and birds that would endanger or threaten the health of the public. Pets that are rejected must be exported or destroyed; the pet will be delivered under customs custody at the port of arrival while waiting disposition at the owner's expense.

Pets imported for one's personal use and not intended for sale may be included in the amount of your customs exemption. If your purchases exceed the amount of your customs exemption, your pet may be imported at the regular rate of duty.

Animals imported for breeding purposes are free of duty under these conditions: A declaration or Customs Form 3327 is required stating that

1. The importer is a citizen of the United States.

2. The animal is imported for breeding purposes.

3. The animal is identical with the description in the certificate of pedigree presented.

Vaccinations

Cats. As a general rule, vaccination against rabies is not required, but they are subject to inspection by a quarantine officer at the port of arrival. If the animal is not in apparent good health, further examination by a licensed veterinarian may be requested at the expense of the owner.

Dogs are subject to vaccination and will not be admitted until they are vaccinated. The owner will be required to arrange and bear the expense of vaccination.

Monkeys must be inspected by a quarantine officer at the port of arrival; a vaccination against rabies is not required.

Food, Drug and Cosmetic Act (Health, Education and Welfare)

All foods, drugs, cosmetics, and therapeutic devices imported into the United States are subject to the same requirements under the act as are products manufactured in the United States and shipped from one state to another. Such products are subject to inspection by the Food and Drug Administration of the Department of Health, Education, and Welfare at the time of entry to determine compliance with the provisions of this law. The inspections are made while the goods are being cleared through customs. Shipments upon examination found not to comply with the act are not entitled to admission into the commerce of the United States.

The United States Food, Drug, and Cosmetic Act does not authorize the Food and Drug Administration to approve foods, drugs, cosmetics, or therapeutic devices, or to pass upon the admissibility of specific lots before they arrive in the United States.

Public Law 87-781, approved October 10, 1962, amending the Federal Food, Drug, and Cosmetic Act, states in part:

The secretary of health, education, and welfare shall furnish to the secretary of the treasury a list of establishments registered and shall request that if any drug manufactured, prepared, compounded, or processed in an establishment not so registered are imported or offered for import into the United States, samples of such drugs should be delivered to the secretary of health, education, and welfare, with notice of such delivery to the owner or consignee, who may appear before the secretary of health, education, and welfare and have the right to introduce testimony.

The Food and Drug Administration is always willing to comment on proposed labels or to answer inquiries from exporters located in foreign countries and from importers in the United States as to the requirements of the law, if such labels or inquiries are accompanied by sufficient information about the foods, drugs, cosmetics, and therapeutic devices and if an adequate description of each ingredient and the quantity of each ingredient in the product is given.

Inquiries may be addressed to the Food and Drug Administration, Department of Health, Education, and Welfare, Washington, D. C. 20204.

Immigration and Nationality Act (Immigration and Naturalization Service)

The function of this service is to collect fees and penalties, withhold clearance of vessels and aircraft subject to imposition of fines for violations of the act; cooperate in dual screening and multiple screening programs; and apprehend and turn over alien stowaways and other illegal aliens who are detected during the course of trying to enter the United States.

Federal Alcohol Administration Act (Bureau of Alcohol, Tobacco and Firearms - ATF)

It enforces compliance with permits, bottling or packaging, labeling and red strip stamping provisions of the act affecting alcohol and products containing distilled spirits. An importer must first obtain an importer's basic permit from the ATF.

A red strip stamp indicating the payment of all Internal Revenue taxes must be affixed to each bottle of imported distilled spirits subject to tax before it can be released from customs custody in the United States. The name and address of the importer must be indelibly overprinted in plain and legible letters on each stamp. The importer may send such stamps abroad to be affixed by the bottler or exporter, or they may be affixed to the containers under customs supervision in a bonded warehouse in the United States before release from customs custody.

Labels affixed to bottles of imported distilled spirits must be covered by certificates of label approval issued to the importer by ATF. Certificates of label approval or photostatic copies thereof required by the regulations of the Internal Revenue Service must be filed with the appropriate customs officer at the port of entry before release may be made of the liquors from customs custody.

National Firearms Act (ATF)

The National Firearms Act establishes enforcement of the prohibition of importation of firearms without licenses.

Request for information regarding importation of alcoholic beverages and firearms should be addressed to the Director, Bureau of Alcohol, Tobacco and Firearms, Department of the Treasury, Washington, D. C. 20226.

Wool Products Labeling Act 1939 (Federal Trade Commission)

Any product containing woolen fiber imported into the United States, with the exception of carpets, rugs, mats, and upholsteries and with the exception of articles made more than twenty years prior to importation, shall be tagged, labeled, or otherwise clearly marked with the following information, as required by the Wool Products Labeling Act of 1939:

1. The percentage of the total fiber weight of the wool product, exclusive of ornamentation not exceeding 5 percent of said total fiber weight of (1) wool; (2) reprocessed wool; (3) reused wool; (4) each fiber other than wool if said percentage by weight of such fiber is 5 percent or more; and

(5) the aggregate of all other fibers.

2. The maximum percentage of the total weight of the wool product of any nonfibrous loading, filling, or adulterating matter.

3. The name of the manufacturer or of the person introducing the product into the commerce of the United States; i.e., the importer. If the importer has a registered identification number issued by the Federal Trade Commission, that number may be used instead of his name.

For the purpose of the enforcement of the Wool Products Labeling Act, a commercial or special customs invoice covering a shipment of wool products exceeding $500 in value and subject to the labeling requirements of the act is required.

The provisions of the Wool Products Labeling Act apply to products manufactured in the United States as well as to imported products.

Flammable Fabrics Act (Federal Trade Commission)

Any article of wearing apparel or interior furnishing or any fabric or related material that is intended for use or that may be used in wearing apparel or interior furnishings cannot be imported into the United States if it fails to conform to an applicable flammability standard issued under Section 4 of the Flammable Fabrics Act.

Such products can be imported into the United States as provided in Section 11(c) of the Flammable Fabrics Act for the purpose of finishing or processing to render such products not so highly flammable as to be dangerous when worn by individuals, provided that the exporter states on the invoice or other paper relating to the shipment that the shipment is being made for that purpose.

The provisions of the Flammable Fabrics Act apply to products manufactured in the United States, as well as to imported products.

Fur Products Labeling Act (Federal Trade Commission)

Labeling requirements. Any article of wearing apparel made in whole or in part of fur or used fur, with the exception of articles that are made of new fur of which the cost or manufacturer's selling price does not exceed seven dollars, imported into the United States shall be tagged, labeled, or

108

otherwise clearly marked to show the following information as required by the Fur Products Labeling Act:

1. The name of the manufacturer or person introducing the product into commerce in the United States, i.e., the importer. If the importer has a registered identification number, that number may be used instead of his name.

2. The name or names of the animal or animals that produced the fur as set forth in the Fur Products Name Guide and as permitted under the rules and regulations.

3. That the fur product contains used fur, when such is the fact.

4. That the fur product is bleached, dyed, or otherwise artificially colored when such is the fact.

5. That the fur product is composed in whole or in substantial part of paws, tails, bellies, or waste fur when such is the fact.

6. The name of the country of origin of any imported furs contained in a fur product.

Invoicing requirements. For the purpose of the enforcement of the Fur Products Labeling Act, a commercial or customs invoice covering a shipment exceeding $500 in value of furs as well as fur products is required.

The provisions of the Fur Products Labeling Act apply to furs and fur products in the United States as well as to imported furs and fur products.

Textile Fiber Products Identification Act (Federal Trade Commission)

Labeling requirements. All textile fiber products imported into the United States shall be stamped, tagged, labeled, or otherwise marked with the following information, as required by the Textile Fiber Products Identification Act, unless exempted from marking under section 12 of the act.

1. The generic names and percentages by weight of the constituent fibers present in the textile fiber product, exclusive of permissive ornamentation, in the amount of more than 5 percent in order of predominance by weight with any percentage of fiber or fibers required to be designated as "other fiber" or "other fibers" appearing last. Fibers present in amounts of 5 percent or less must be designated as "other fibers."

2. The name of the manufacturer, or the name or registered identification number issued by the Federal Trade

Commission of one or more persons marketing or handling the textile fiber product. A word trademark used as a house mark, registered in the United States Patent Office, may be used on labels in lieu of the name otherwise required, if the owner of such trademark furnishes a copy of the registration to the Federal Trade Commission prior to its use.

3. The name of the country where processed or manufactured.

Invoicing requirements. For the purpose of the enforcement of the Textile Fiber Products Identification Act, a commercial or customs invoice covering a shipment of textile fiber products exceeding $500 in value and subject to the labeling requirements of the act is required to show the following information in addition to that ordinarily required on such invoices:

1. The constituent fiber or combination of fibers in the textile fiber product, designating with equal prominence each natural or manufactured fiber in the textile fiber product by its generic name in the order of predominance by the weight thereof if the weight of such fiber is 5 percent or more of the total fiber weight of the product.

2. The percentage of each fiber present, by weight, in the total fiber content of the textile fiber product, exclusive of ornamentation not exceeding 5 percent by weight of the total fiber content.

3. The name, or other identification issued and registered by the Federal Trade Commission, of the manufacturer of the product or one or more persons marketing or handling the textile fiber product.

4. The name of the country where processed or manufactured.

The provisions of the Textile Fiber Products Identification Act apply to textile fiber products manufactured in the United States as well as to imported products.

Copyright Act (Library of Congress)

The first federal copyright law was initiated May 31, 1790, and protected maps, charts, and books. The term was fourteen years with the privilege of renewal for fourteen years. February 3, 1831, marked the first general revision of the copyright law. Music was added to the protected works. The term of copyright was extended to twenty-eight years with

110

privilege of renewal for fourteen years. The third general revision (March 4, 1909) of the copyright law is the basis of the present law. The date of copyright was changed to the date of publication for published works. The renewal term was extended to twenty-eight years, and then to public domain. September 16, 1955, was the effective date of the Universal Copyright Convention and related changes.

Copyright protection embraces many different articles, e.g., pamphlets, periodicals, music, photographic works, prints, pictorial illustrations, and many others.

The principal function of the Copyright Office is to register copyright claims. Important provisions of the copyright law are enforced by the U. S. Customs Service wherein they may prohibit or limit the kind or quantity of books that may be brought into the United States.

Public Law 89-651 was signed by President Johnson on October 14, 1966, the United States implementation of its adherence to the UNESCO's Florence Agreement. The new law provides duty-free importation for four categories of articles: printed matter; books not specially provided for; music in books and sheets; and maps, atlases and charts (with some exceptions, notably tourist literature and printed matter not specially provided for suitable use in the production of such books as would themselves be free of duty). Sheets and other parts for books also were made free of duty.

The United States implementation of a parallel UNESCO pact, the Beirut Agreement by Presidential Proclamation, went into effect January 1, 1967. This abolished duties on the audio-visual material of an educational, scientific, or cultural nature being imported for nonprofit educational purposes. Such material was treated conditionally free if the importer could satisfy the district director with the provisions of Item 870.30 of the Tariff Act of 1930, as amended, embracing these matters, if he filed with the entry covering such articles a document issued by the United States Information Agency certifying that the articles are visual or auditory materials of an educational, scientific, or cultural nature. In the event that the district director of customs at the port of entry does not receive the document within a ninety-day period, the merchandise shall be immediately classified and liquidated without regard to Item 870.30.

Although the Florence agreement made books in the English language containing textual matter free of duty, it has no bearing on the copyright issue, which will be enforced by the customs authorities.

The "manufacturing clause" of the copyright law requires that books be manufactured in the United States (typesetting, printing, and binding) as a condition of copyright.

When a book by an American citizen or domicilary has been manufactured and copyrighted, in the United States the importation of foreign manufactured reprints is prohibited.

In April, 1974, the customs authorities made the following provisions in the customs regulations requesting additional information for certain classes of merchandise. Invoices for books shall set forth the additional information specifying:

1. The name of the shipper (or seller) and the importer.

2. The title and quantity of each title imported.

3. The unit price for each book.

4. The form of the copyright notice printed in the book (if none, state "no copyright notice"), e.g., © John Doe 1975.

5. If the book bears a copyright notice the following information is required:

(a) The country in which the book was first published.

(b) The citizenship of the author on the date of first publication.

(c) Whether the author was domiciled in the United States on the date of first publication.

The above information must be presented to customs at the time of entry.

Books may be imported in unlimited quantities and no import statement is required if:

(a) The country in which the book was first published is a Universal Copyright Convention country; or

(b) The country of which the author is a citizen is a convention country; provided the author is neither a United States citizen nor domicilary, and provided the work was not first published in the United States.

If the book is written by an American author and is published abroad, it must be registered for an ad interim copyright and in the United States Library of Congress, and there is a 1,500 copy limit on importation to the United States within a period of five years of the first publication. An import statement from the Library of Congress (for copyright purposes) should be attached to the commercial invoice and forwarded to the broker at the time of entry. Should the import statement not be available, then the broker can obtain a bond for a missing document to be furnished within a period of six months.

If the author of a copyright work is a foreign citizen and is domiciled in the United States, an "import statement" is necessary.

When the registrant of a copyright is a foreign publisher and the author is an American, and it is a work for hire, the foreign publisher or registrant is deemed to be constructively the author for copyright purposes.

False notice of copyright. If a book bears the legend or the imprint "© John Doe 1975" and the author is an American citizen, and if an ad interim copyright is not obtained by the registrant from the Library of Congress Copyright Office in Washington, the importer has two alternatives. He may export the books to the country of origin or else obtain permission from the registrant to obliterate the copyright notice, otherwise they will be subject to seizure and forfeiture. In the event the importer has disposed of the books, he will be liable for liquidated damages.

Piratical copies.

(a) Definition. Piratical copies are actual copies or substantial copies of a recorded copyrighted work, produced and imported in contravention of the rights of the copyright owner.

(b) Importation prohibited. The importation of piratical copies of works copyrighted in the United States is prohibited.

(c) Seizure and forfeiture. The district director shall seize and forfeit an imported article that he determines constitutes a piratical copy of a recorded copyrighted work. The district director shall also seize and forfeit an imported article if the importer does not deny a representation that the article is a piratical copy.

The new copyright law is still pending. Some of the changes sought are:

1. The extension of the copyright protection for the life of the author plus fifty years after death.

2. Relaxation of a requirement that a book must be printed in this country to qualify for United States copyright protection. The bill would retain the concept of the manufacturing clause, i.e., that for works of American authorship, domestic manufacture is a precondition for copyright protection. However, it would

do so in such a way that domestic printing done from imported reproduction proofs would not jeopardize copyright protection.

3. The bill would raise the number of copies of a United States author's foreign produced edition that could be imported from the present 1,500 to 2,000 copies.

4. "Fair use" would be left to the courts to decide the issue of infringement. The factors to be considered:

    a. The purpose and character of the use.

    b. The nature of the copyrighted work.

    c. The amount and substantiality of the portion used in relation to the copyrighted work as a whole.

    d. The effect of the use upon the potential market for or value of the copyrighted work.

The countries presently adhering to the Universal Copyright Convention are Andorra, Argentina, Australia, Austria, Belgium, Brazil, Cambodia, Canada, Chile, Costa Rica, Cuba, Czechoslovakia, Denmark, Ecuador, Fiji, Finland, France, German Federal Republic, Ghana, Greece, Guatemala, Haiti, Holy See, Hungary, Iceland, India, Ireland, Israel, Italy, Japan, Kenya, Laos, Lebanon, Liberia, Liechtenstein, Luxembourg, Malawi, Malta, Mauritius, Mexico, Monaco, Morocco, Netherlands, New Zealand, Nicaragua, Nigeria, Norway, Pakistan, Panama, Paraguay, Peru, Philippines, Portugal, Spain, Sweden, Switzerland, Tunisia, Union of Soviet Socialist Republics, United Kingdom, United States of America, Venezuela, Yugoslavia, and Zambia.

Trademark Act (Department of Commerce)

It shall be unlawful to import into the United States merchandise bearing an American trademark or any merchandise of foreign importation if such merchandise, or the label, sign, print package, wrapper or receptacle bears a trademark owned by a citizen of, or by a corporation or association organized in the United States and registered in the Patent Office by a person domiciled in the United States and if the copy of the certificate of registration of such trademark is filed with the secretary of the treasury, unless written consent of the owner of such trademark is produced at the time of making entry.

After recording his trade name or trademark with customs, the owner thereof is given the protection against the importation by others of foreign merchandise of any illegal or unauthorized names or marks.

Should there be a change in the name of the owner of a recorded trademark, but no change in ownership, written notice thereof shall be given to the commissioner of customs accompanied by a status copy of the certificate of registration certified by the United States Patent Office showing title to be presently in the name as changed and the usual fee payable to the United States Customs Service.

To protect the trademark owner for the recording of a written application, he shall submit it not later than three months after the date of expiration of the current twenty-year trademark registration issued by the Patent Office.

There is a restriction on the importation of certain types of articles such as cameras, binoculars, perfumes, jewelry, and other articles from various countries because the American ownership of the trademark has been assigned to a person or corporation in the United States. The foreign manufacturer's trademarked products, including articles purchased for personal use may not be imported without the consent of the American trademark owner who is the only one entitled to use the trademark in the United States.

Any such merchandise imported in the United States in violation thereof shall be subject to seizure or forfeiture for violation of the customs laws or the importer may be required to export or destroy such merchandise or to remove or obliterate such trademark and shall be liable for the wrongful use of the trademark.

Chapter 19

SMUGGLING

Smuggling is a word that is closely linked with the United States Customs Service. Why do people try to smuggle diamonds, watches, jewelry, art work, antiques, and other articles? The answer should be quite obvious--to avoid paying the import duty as well as income tax. How about drugs such as heroin, cocaine, and marihuana? Because narcotics are prohibited, smugglers must contrive ways and means resorting to clandestine methods to foil the customs authorities.

Drug abuse has become one of our outstanding problems in the United States and the Treasury Department is trying to combat the illicit traffic of dangerous drugs. The modus operandi is very interesting and cleverly organized by the smugglers. The only one who carries the merchandise is ordinarily a paid carrier and the key men of any ring never carry anything suspicious. Should the carrier run into difficulty, there are a group of men detailed to come to his assistance at some stage of the operation.

Smuggling, like any other business, is a specialized field. The syndicate or average smuggler is very cautious not to employ any carrier with a criminal record. The smuggler is a cautious fellow and does not deal with people with whom he does not share matters in common.

There are many avenues from whom customs obtains information, e.g., disgruntled employees, racketeers, businessmen, ships' officers, stewards, and others. Some relate for fear they will be deported, or fear of a severe prison sentence, or fear that unless they get the law on their side, their underworld enemies will annihilate them.

Informer's Compensation

It is quite rewarding for informants. Informers are those persons who are not officers of the United States government but who give the first information to the government of a violation of law. This information leads to prosecution and contributes to the conviction of the offender or the recovery of a fine, penalty, or forfeiture. However, it does not apply when seizure and forfeiture is made under the Internal Revenue law.

Claimants may be paid 25 percent of the net amount received from duties withheld or any fine, penalty, or forfeiture incurred, but such amount shall not exceed $50,000 regardless of the number of recoveries growing out of the information furnished.

While it is true that awareness by bounty hunters may be misapplied at times to the smuggling of articles by passengers, it may lead to embarrassment by the customs, particularly where the suspected smuggler is innocent and the charge is invalid. However, all matters are given due consideration and customs must continue its close scrutiny for smugglers.

As for the importation of drugs into this country, the United States Customs Service checks contraband by means of electronics, international cooperation, interagencies, cooperation of private citizens, informants and more recently, detector dogs.

The Customs Service has achieved a very outstanding record on drug seizures due to its keen observation and intelligence exercised with incoming passengers at the ports of entry and along our borders.

In July, 1973, there was a consolidation of the drug abuse enforcement agencies with the Justice Department known as the Drug Enforcement Administration (DEA). Some of the customs agents were transferred to the DEA. However, drug seizures by the Customs Service are turned over to DEA agents for investigation.

Chapter 20

CONTROVERSIAL ISSUES

Import Quotas

An import quota is a quantity control in imported merchandise for a certain period of time.

The Burke-Hartke bill endorsed by the members of A.F.L.-C.I.O. believed that the Foreign Trade and Investment Act of 1972 would be a way to protect the American economy and jobs by restricting imports and causing difficulty with the operations of American owned companies abroad. It was contended that "buying American" would lower prices since duty has to be paid on imported merchandise, which would increase the cost of goods. Further, it would give opportunities for employment to our people.

If we discriminate against imports, it is only logical that other countries will act in similar fashion against American exports. Some outstanding economists believe that imports are the only real competition for many American firms. The consumer benefits from the competition in price and quality. The American firms gain because they are motivated to increase their productivity, for markets both at home and abroad.

Liberalization has been the trend the past two decades when President Roosevelt requested Congress for permission to negotiate reciprocal tariff reductions with other countries, resulting in the First Reciprocal Trade Agreement Act, which was adopted in 1934-1967. This was further manifested with the Kennedy Round-Up under the General Agreement of Tariff and Trade (G.A.T.T.) wherein there were reduced rates on importations year after year until 1972.

Arts

Customs regulations pertaining to purchases by an individual for his own use require that paintings, drawings, and sketches claimed to be duty free according to the tariff be accompanied by a declaration from the artist, seller, or shipper to the effect that such merchandise is original.

Under the tariff act "original" does not necessarily mean "one of a kind." Item 765.03 embraces paintings, pastels, drawings, and sketches, all the foregoing whether or not originals, executed wholly by hand. Item 765.10 provides for duty free entry of etchings, engravings, woodcuts, lithographs, and prints made by other hand transfer processes. It further defines such prints to include only such as are printed by hand from plates, stones, or blocks etched, drawn or engraved with hand tools and not such as are printed from plates, stones, or blocks etched, drawn or engraved by photochemical or other mechanical processes.

Item 765.15 defines original sculpture and statuary to include professional production of sculpture only, as distinguished from artisans. It is also defined to refer to the original model and not more than ten castings, replicas, or productions made from the sculptor's original work or model with or without a change in scale regardless of whether or not the sculptor is alive at the time the castings, replicas, or reproductions are completed. Item 765.20 covers original mosaics. Item 765.30 embraces works of art that are productions of American artists residing temporarily abroad.

Sculpture in this classification should not be confused with the varieties of commercially produced figurines and ornamental objects popular with tourists.

The problem of the import specialist in the classification of "art" is rather intricate and involved. Certain metallic objects have been imported and have been characterized as objets d'art by the importer whereas the eye of the customs import specialist or the inspector could not accept such creativity as being works of art because they did not represent any definite object despite their symmetry or ornamentation. After many discussions this matter was taken to the U. S. Customs Court where it was held in behalf of the importer.

Obscenity

The prevailing idea is that there is no legally workable definition of obscenity. It is a matter of distinguishing erotic realism and hard-core pornography. Each case stands on its own merits. The yardstick is "prurient issues" and if prurient, the material may be dangerous to a "young person" or a "susceptible reader."

The Supreme Court has stated that sex and obscenity

are not the same. The portrayal of sex in art, literature, and scientific works is not in itself sufficient reason to deny the material the protection of the Constitution for freedom of the press. Kinsey's Report on Sexual Behavior, which was consigned to the Institute of Sex Research at Indiana University, was not permitted entry into the United States by customs. The reasons were that the material was pornographic. There was a test case in court and it was held that since the material was intended for scientific use, the statute barring pornography did not apply.

Another interesting case, decided by the court, was that of Ulysses, by James Joyce. U.S. Customs likewise rejected its entry into the United States. It was taken to court and decided in favor of the appellant. The highlight of that case was that the book must be read in its entirety and three outstanding factors were deduced from this ruling: the intention of the author, the pornography, and the ultimate reader.

It seems the trend is changing as to what constitutes pornography, which is evidenced by the reversals of some of the rulings regarding titles that until recently were deemed to be violations of Section 305 of the Tariff Act of 1930, as amended. Some of these titles were the unexpurgated version of Lady Chatterley's Lover, by D. H. Lawrence; Tropic of Cancer, and Tropic of Capricorn, by Henry Miller. Others are too numerous to mention.

In these cases, the First and Fourteenth Amendments to the U.S. Constitution were invoked. The First Amendment provides in part: "Congress shall make no law respecting an establishment of religion, or prohibiting the free exercise thereof; or abridging the freedom of speech, or of the press. . . ."

The Fourteenth Amendment provides in part: "No state shall . . . deprive any person of life, liberty or property, without due process of law; nor deny to any person within its jurisdiction the equal protection of the laws."

The American Law Institute in trying to establish a model penal code defined "obscenity" as follows: A thing is obscene, if, considered as a whole, the predominant appeal is to prurient interest in nudity, sex or excretion, and if it goes substantially beyond customary limits of candor in description or representation of such materials."

Based on this logic, the thinking of the Supreme Court advises that material appealing to prurient interest is "material having a tendency to excite lustful thoughts."

120

According to court decisions as to the importation of books, obscenity is not a technical term of the law and is not susceptible of exact definition.

Furniture

The provision of law prescribed by customs within the tariff act makes it very difficult for the import specialist to determine the authenticity of an imported article as to the year of its production despite the declaration of the supplier. There must be a further determination by the import specialist to ascertain whether the antique has been repaired to the extent that a substantial amount of material has been added to make that portion dutiable despite the fact that the article was produced prior to 100 years before entry. Where the original article was so changed as to lose its identity, it is excluded from free entry and the entire article is dutiable.

Silverware

The import specialist's job becomes very difficult where subterfuge is used by the supplier to make an article appear to be an antique. Hallmarks are important factors in determining genuineness. A transfer of a famous hallmark from a small piece of silver to another article, such as a tray, is a common practice. Another method of forgery is to make a cast of an old piece of silver and from the casting create a duplicate. Although the new silver piece looks aged, the patina is artificial. The import specialist has the expertise and the knowledge that the patina of the old silver manifests a mellow coloration due to the time element.

There is an additional duty of 12.5 percent on imports from most favored nations, and 25 percent on imports from communist countries, imposed by the tariff schedules of the United States, of any article that is imported for sale and claimed to be free of duty as an antique, at the time of entry or at a later date, and found to be unauthentic as to antiquity. However, the claim can be withdrawn in writing before the examination has begun of the article for the purpose of appraisement or classification.

Appendix
Trade Act of 1974
Generalized System of Preferences

On November 24, 1975, the President of the United States issued an Executive Order #11888 implementing the Generalized System of Preferences effective January 1, 1976, which authorized the establishment of preferences for eligible articles imported from beneficiary developing countries. *This applies to regular shipments, mail shipments, travelers or tourist purchases from the beneficiary developing countries stated herein.* It does not apply to non-beneficiary developing countries and territories. It does not affect the present rates applicable to the most favored nations or communist countries.

"G.S.P." or Generalized System of Preferences has been a world wide effort on the part of industrialized countries to help developing countries known as "Beneficiary Developing Countries" to grow industrially and agriculturally in world trade. The United States has agreed to allow duty-free entry for certain specific products from certain specific countries designated as beneficiary developing countries. These products are to be duty-free from all countries on the list, with few exceptions. *As there are more than two thousand products on the Presidential list they are too numerous to mention.* (Should you wish to obtain information as to these items contact the U.S. Customs Service at your respective port.)

The following is a list of beneficiary developing countries:

Afghanistan, Angola, Argentina, Bahamas, Bahrain, Bangladesh, Barbados, Bhutan, Bolivia, Botswana, Brazil, Burma, Burundi, Cameroon, Cape Verde, Central African Republic, Chad, Chile, Colombia, Congo (Brazzaville), Costa Rica, Cyprus, Dahomey, Dominican Republic, Egypt, El Salvador, Equatorial Guinea, Ethiopia, Fiji, Gambia, Ghana, Grenada, Guatemala, Guinea, Guinea Bissau, Guyana, Haiti, Honduras, India, Israel, Ivory Coast, Jamaica, Jordan, Kenya, Republic of Korea, Laos, Lebanon, Lesotho, Liberia, Malagasy Republic, Malawi, Malaysia, Maldive Islands, Mali, Malta, Mauritania, Mauritius, Mexico, Morocco, Mozambique, Nauru, Nepal, Nicaragua, Niger, Oman, Pakistan, Panama, Papua, New Guinea, Paraguay, Peru, Philippines, Romania, Rwanda, Sao Tome and Principe, Senegal, Sierra Leone, Singapore, Somalia, Sri Lanka, Sudan, Surinam, Swaziland, Syria, Taiwan, Tanzania, Thailand, Togo, Tonga, Trinidad and Tobago, Tunisia, Turkey, Upper Volta, Uruguay, Western Samoa, Yemen Arab Republic, Yugoslavia, Zaire, Zambia.

Requisites In order to be eligible, goods must:

(1) be on the list of products in the Presidential order;

(2) must be wholly the growth, product or manufacture of the beneficiary country, or have not less than 35 percent of the United States appraised value added in the beneficiary country. The sum of the cost or value of the materials produced in the beneficiary country, plus the direct costs of processing operations performed in such country constitute the value to be used in computing the 35 percent.

(3) Must not be on the list of specifically excluded products from specific countries which is part of the Presidential order.

If the product is not wholly the product of the beneficiary country, it must be "substantially transformed in the beneficiary developing country into a new and different article of commerce" from any material, part, component or product imported into the beneficiary country. The product must be shipped directly from the beneficiary country to the United States. If the shipment passes through another country on the way to the United States, all shipping documents must show the United States as the final destination and the goods must not enter into the commerce of any other country. The United States Customs Service may require proof (shipping documents) of direct shipment, but such proof is not routinely required with the entry. The importer will have sixty days to produce proof if required.

There are three ways in which a product can be removed from the list:

(a) Should a single beneficiary country ship more than $25,000,000 of a beneficiary product into the United States in a year, that product will be removed from the list, for that country, in the following year. The total amount will be adjusted each year in accordance with the United States Gross National Product.

(b) No single beneficiary country may ship more than 50 percent of all United States imports in one year of a single beneficiary product to the United States, or it will be removed from the list the following year.

(c) The President may remove a country or a product, or a specific product from a specific country from the list at any time, by proclamation for violation of these conditions.

Procedures   A "claim" must be made for duty-free entry at the time of entry or Immediate Delivery (I.D.) Application, and before customs releases the goods. Placing the letter "A" before the Tariff Schedules of the United States (TSUS) number on the consumption entry or I.D. Application will constitute the necessary claim according to customs.

A certificate of origin must be filed for every shipment of eligible merchandise valued at more than $250.00. The certificate which will be known as "Form A" must be signed by the exporter and certified by the government of the exporting country. "Form A" is an internationally agreed upon and universally used document.

If the certificate of origin is lost, stolen, or destroyed, a duplicate may be filed with the entry or I.D. Application. The duplicate must be issued by the foreign government, and must be endorsed with the word "duplicate."

If the certificate of origin is missing, entry will be permitted under bond. Unless extended by customs, sixty days will be allowed in which to produce the missing document. Liquidated damages may be imposed for failure to furnish "Form A."

Shipments and tourist purchases of less than $250 in value do not require a certificate of origin for duty-free treatment but U.S. Customs Service can and may require other proof of origin.

Effective date of the Generalized System of Preferences (G.S.P.)   Goods must have been both imported and entered for consumption on or after January 1, 1976. If goods were placed in a warehouse before January 1, 1976, they will not be admitted duty-free.